FIGHTING EVIL

Recent Titles in
Contributions to the Study of World Literature

Aspects and Issues in the History of Children's Literature
Maria Nikolajeva, editor

Reluctant Expatriate: The Life of Harold Frederic
Robert M. Myers

The Decline of the Goddess: Nature, Culture, and Women in Thomas Hardy's
Fiction
Shirley A. Stave

Postcolonial Discourse and Changing Cultural Contexts
Gita Rajan and Radhika Mohanram, editors

Prometheus and Faust: The Promethean Revolt in Drama from Classical
Antiquity to Goethe
Timothy Richard Wutrich

English Postcoloniality: Literatures from Around the World
Radhika Mohanram and Gita Rajan, editors

The Vonnegut Chronicles
Peter Reed and Marc Leeds, editors

Satirical Apocalypse: An Anatomy of Melville's *The Confidence-Man*
Jonathan A. Cook

Twenty-Four Ways of Looking at Mary McCarthy: The Writer and Her Work
Eve Stwertka and Margo Viscusi, editors

Orienting Masculinity, Orienting Nation: W. Somerset Maugham's Exotic
Fiction
Philip Holden

A Matter of Faith: The Fiction of Brian Moore
Robert Sullivan

Samuel Johnson and the Essay
Robert D. Spector

FIGHTING EVIL

Unsung Heroes in the Novels of Graham Greene

Haim Gordon

Contributions to the Study of World Literature, Number 73

GREENWOOD PRESS
Westport, Connecticut • London

Library of Congress Cataloging-in-Publication Data

Gordon, Hayim.
  Fighting evil : unsung heroes in the novels of Graham Greene /
Haim Gordon.
     p.   cm. —(Contributions to the study of world literature,
  ISSN 0738–9345 ; no. 73)
  Includes bibliographical references (p.   ) and index.
  ISBN 0–313–29574–3 (alk. paper)
  1. Greene, Graham, 1904– —Characters—Heroes. 2. Didactic
fiction, English—History and criticism. 3. Good and evil in
literature. 4. Heroes in literature. I. Title. II. Series.
PR6013.R44Z63344 1997
823′.912—dc20   96–22006

British Library Cataloguing in Publication Data is available.

Library of Congress Catalog Card Number: 96–22006
ISBN: 0–313–29574–3
ISSN: 0738–9345

First published in 1997

Greenwood Press, 88 Post Road West, Westport, CT 06881
An imprint of Greenwood Publishing Group, Inc.

Printed in the United States of America

The paper used in this book complies with the
Permanent Paper Standard issued by the National
Information Standards Organization (Z39.48–1984).

10 9 8 7 6 5 4 3 2 1

For Noam Chomsky
Thanks for everything you have taught me

Contents

Acknowledgments   ix

Introduction   1

PART I: EVIL   9

1   Manipulative Evil   11

2   Greed and Lust for Power   23

3   Political Evil   33

4   Fanaticism   45

PART II: UNSUNG HEROES WHO FIGHT EVIL   53

5   Seeing Evil   55

6   Simple Courage and Trust in the World   65

7   Sensitivity to Horror   75

8   Failure and Integrity   85

PART III: THE WISDOM OF UNSUNG HEROES   97

9   Comedians and Tragedy   99

10   Existential Wisdom: Joy, Courage, Questioning   111

11   Political Wisdom: Power and Glory   121

Contents

12 Conclusion: Learning to Fight Evil   127
Selected Bibliography   131
Index   135

Acknowledgments

Much of my life has been involved in writing this study of fighting evil and Graham Greene's novels. Hence, all those people who have, in many ways, shared my own fights with evil or supported those fights genuinely share in this modest volume. I have learned much from them and their efforts, and, although I cannot list them all, I cherish the memories of our working together. The ongoing support of Harold and Myra Shapiro has always encouraged me in my attempts to fight evil. Leonard Grob has again and again confirmed my efforts to halt evil, as have my children, Nitzan, Mor, and Neve. Above all, my wife Rivca has been a constant, loving partner, whose penetrating wisdom and faithful help I cannot ever hope to evaluate. Thanks to all of you.

FIGHTING EVIL

Introduction

Ballads will probably never be sung about the characters in Graham Greene's novels who fight evil. Greene recognized that, in the contemporary world, in which we are persistently indoctrinated to applaud celebrity and financial success, many courageous people who fight evil and struggle for justice are short-changed. Their stories remain untold, unremembered. Those whom he describes fighting evil are not knights or generals, hard-nosed detectives, clever sleuths, or lauded political leaders. They are simple people whom one may meet in a bar or encounter coming out of a cinema. They themselves may have often acted wrongly or been manipulated by others to participate in doing evil. Yet, at a certain moment, they have seen specific evils for what they are and have decided to stand up for the good. They choose to do what is right. Let me say it again: They are courageous.

They are also sensitive people who care for others, who are attracted to a worthy life, who search for love in a world in which the destruction of human freedom, alienation, brutal oppression, and greedy exploitation prevail. These unsung heroes recognize that many of the evils they encounter are performed and supported by wicked governments and by seemingly innocent ordinary people. Throughout his novels, Greene repeatedly unmasks these evildoers, showing us their true ugly faces.

Greene's unsung heroes also perceive, but rarely articulate, that they will attain personal integrity only by quietly abandoning the crowd, with its indifference to the horrors of evil and human suffering. There is an educational message here. Greene reveals to us, his readers, that the difficult struggle against evil is a possibility open to simple people like ourselves. If we decide to engage in such a fight, we will often attain integrity. Put differently, Greene's unsung heroes teach us this lesson: The difficult challenge of fighting the evil and the evildoers we encounter daily is a laudable commitment—and we, too, can participate in such a commendable undertaking.

I should add immediately that Greene's vivid portrayals of simple people who fight evil attracted me to his novels. More than scholarly interest nourishes this attraction. For many years, in the modest ways available to me, I have tried, together with other Israelis, to fight some of the instances of evil that have flourished here in Israel. We simple persons have fought evils such as Israel's brutal oppression of the Palestinians, the de facto denial of equal rights for women in Israel, and the supposedly subtle restricting of free speech and thought in Israeli educational institutions.

For the course of this book, my experience leads me to accept a definition of evil, based on Jean-Paul Sartre's philosophy, that I believe Greene would willingly endorse: Evil is any willful destruction of human freedom. This definition includes killing, raping, molesting, torturing, oppressing, inflicting suffering, exploiting, and many other ways of destroying a person's freedom. Thus, in accordance with Sartre's thought, human freedom should be grasped in its broadest possible sense—Sartre held that a person *is* freedom. Sartre's definition includes examples such as the political evil instigated by the French and U.S. governments and performed by their armies and diplomats in Vietnam and Indochina, or the evils of General Alfredo Stroessner in Paraguay and of President Luis Somoza in Nicaragua. It also includes the harsh oppression of Palestinians by the Israeli army. Of course, this definition of evil includes the wickedness of crooks like Pinkie in *Brighton Rock* and of fanatics like Rycker in *A Burnt-Out Case*.

Note that Sartre's definition of evil is also broad enough to include acts such as the pollution of the earth and its natural resources. It is evident, for instance, that the terrible air pollution in Mexico City destroys the life and hence the freedom of many Mexicans. As hundreds of scientific studies have concluded, our children's life and freedom will be endangered, impaired, and perhaps ruined by the air, water, and land that we currently pollute. It should be mentioned, however, that the evil that Graham Greene describes is usually the direct destruction of human freedom by evildoers such as the Tontons Macoute in Haiti in *The Comedians*, or the CIA agent, Quigly, in *The Captain and the Enemy*, or the lieutenant in *The Power and the Glory*.

～

In choosing simple, unsung heroes as central characters of his novels, in deciding to involve the reader in the lives of people like Ida in *Brighton Rock*, the whiskey priest in *The Power and the Glory*, Brown in *The Comedians*, Thomas Fowler in *The Quiet American*, or D. and Rose Cullen in *The Confidential Agent*, Graham Greene is quite exceptional. What exactly is Greene's uniqueness?

In contemporary literature, the detailed difficulties and challenges that a simple person may encounter in fighting evil and the courageous possibilities open to those willing to do so have seldom been articulated. Marcel Proust, William Faulkner, Albert Camus, Saul Bellow, Virginia Woolf, and Thomas Mann, to mention a few—none of these authors has described in detail the daily difficulties of struggling against the many evil regimes and evil people that have often triumphed during the twentieth century. There are a few exceptions. Robert Jordan in Ernest Hemingway's *For Whom the Bell Tolls* comes to mind. But such exceptions only strengthen the fact that very few unsung heroes, like the whiskey priest in *The Power and the Glory* or Dr. Czinner in *Stamboul Train*, populate the novels of these and other great writers. In twentieth-century literature, Graham Greene's unsung heroes seem to be a special group of simple people who have rarely been portrayed. Not being portrayed has resulted in the fact that, in literature, such unsung heroes have hardly ever attained the glory they deserve.

Scholars of Graham Greene, or of twentieth-century literature more generally, have been not at all attracted to the theme of fighting evil, or to the lives and struggles of the simple people who fight evil and who repeatedly appear in Greene's novels. Of the thirty-eight books currently in print that deal with Greene's writings, not one professes to examine the relevance of Greene's novels, and especially his unsung heroes, for fighting evil; nor have I found a journal article that deals with this theme.

Unfortunately, these scholars are following a general trend. Evil and the need to fight it have pretty much been banished from scholarly and popular discussions. Bourgeois politicians, their faithful bureaucrats, and many highly praised scholars who act as educated servants of the regime never acknowledge the existence of evil; at most they are willing to admit that there are "tensions in the system." It has been pointed out that the banishing of evil from almost all popular and scholarly discussions owes much to the superficiality spread by psychologists and other social scientists, who deal with feelings or with general statistical data, not with human freedom and deeds. I have discussed this trend and its shallowness, happily embraced by many evildoers and their well-educated spokespersons, in a recent book. There I explained at length that the refusal by academics, politicians, social scientists, and many others to discuss evil is both wrong and cowardly.[1] Such a refusal implicitly supports the evildoers, who fear exposure.

As the reader will learn from what follows, such behavior by academics, especially by those who write about Graham Greene, often enrages me. I should perhaps add that my discussion of the support of evil by academics accords with various ideas that appear in Greene's novels. For instance, in *It's a Battlefield*, Greene ridicules and reveals the hollowness of the shallow academics, careerist politicians, public officials, inane journalists, and narrow-minded bureaucrats who, by their choice of stupidity, myopia, banality, and indifference, support evil.

From a historical perspective, the refusal of academics to see evil creates a sad and paradoxical situation. In this terrible twentieth century, which has witnessed, among other evils, the Nazi Holocaust, the killing of millions of kulaks in the Soviet Union, the destruction of millions of Chinese lives during a so-called cultural revolution, the killing of 2 million Vietnamese by the United States in a war of aggression; in this century, in which many millions of people still rot away in gulags and which must confess many so-called "small" genocides, such as that of the Armenians or lately those in Rwanda; yes, in this century of atrocities, with the continuing slave labor of tens of millions of Third World inhabitants, with its political evil cynically performed by the Nazi SS and the American CIA and the Soviet KGB, as well as by the Tontons Macoute, the brown shirts, the Ku Klux Klan, the red guards, and many other wicked organizations—in this century, in which so much evil has occurred and is still occurring, the large majority of writers and scholars prefer to never address the problem of evil. And since, unlike Graham Greene, they refuse to see evil and to brand it for what it is, they have nothing to tell us about how to fight the evil that we encounter in our day-to-day existence.

There are important exceptions; the authors Heinrich Böll and Aleksandr Solzhenitsyn come to mind, as do the philosophers Noam Chomsky and Jean-Paul Sartre. And there is a small but significant group of scholars who do describe and brand evil people and organizations for their vile deeds.[2] Still, Graham Greene is unique. Because neither Böll, nor Solzhenitsyn, nor any other authors I know have presented a large group of unsung heroes in many novels, heroes with backgrounds and approaches to life as diverse as those of Ida Arnold in *Brighton Rock* and Thomas Fowler in *The Quiet American*, who decide to fight evil for the simple reason that it *is* evil—and that it is our responsibility to erase evil from the face of the earth.

It is indeed unfortunate that my discussion of Graham Greene's unsung heroes has not been able to learn from contemporary literary scholarship. As indicated, this broad field of study pretty much overlooks the existence of evil in the world. Moreover, many literary scholars seem deliberately to ignore the message of realistic novels, such as those written by Greene, in which evil is prominent and the need to fight it calls to the reader. Need I add that such a confining of the field of literary scholarship greatly limits the depth and the insights that these scholars can provide? Describing and discussing the sad situation of contemporary literary scholarship is beyond the scope of this book. Nonetheless, a few striking examples of the myopia of literary scholars who have written about Greene's novels and have ignored the existence of evil appear in some chapters of this study. I will not conceal my indignation and revulsion toward the writings of those scholars who ignore the widespread existence of evil in the world—evil that repeatedly appears in Greene's novels.

In the twentieth century, it has been mainly existentialist philosophers and theologians, as well as some political philosophers and historians, who have addressed, analyzed, and discussed the widespread evil that prevails. Here and there you will find a poet (for instance, Pablo Neruda), a playwright (think of Jean Genet), or a few novelists, such as those mentioned above, who poignantly portray evil and indicate the need to fight it. But they are very rare. Many discussions in this book, therefore, will be based primarily on the thought and insights of existentialist writers—Martin Buber, Martin Heidegger, Jean-Paul Sartre, and others—and of political thinkers and historians such as Noam Chomsky and Hannah Arendt. Here and there I will also rely on the wisdom of ancient and modern philosophers. It should not come as a surprise that I will repeatedly attack the political philosophy of Thomas Hobbes who brilliantly presented the philosophical basis for a bourgeois mode of existence.

In considering Greene's novels with the help of existentialist philosophy, this book will support a view that has been partially accepted. Quite a few scholars have, correctly in my view, pointed out that Graham Greene's writings present themes that are very close to writings of major existentialists: Heidegger, Sartre,

Camus, and Søren Kierkegaard. Other scholars have gone further and listed Greene explicitly as an existentialist. One scholarly monograph has compared Greene to the Spanish philosopher, Miguel de Unamuno, another to Kierkegaard.

~

Graham Greene's unsung heroes face many manifestations of evil. In Part I of this book, I list these manifestations under four major categories that very often overlap and support each other: manipulative evil; greed and lust for power; political evil; and fanaticism. The categories are discussed separately, while some indications of how they interact are presented.

Manipulative evil emerges when a person, through manipulation, insidiously and purposely destroys the freedom of other persons, very often for his or her own immediate gain. This situation can occur both on the interpersonal level and in the political realm. Thus, manipulative evil often appears together with political evil; think of Alden Pyle in Greene's *The Quiet American*. Several cases of manipulative evil resemble that of Aunt Augusta in *Travels with my Aunt*; it has a rather indirect relation to politics. Manipulative evil with hardly any political implications is found in the deeds of Pinkie in *Brighton Rock* and of Rycker in *A Burnt-Out Case*.

Part I dwells on what can be learned from the manipulative evil, the greed and lust for power, the political evil, and the fanaticism portrayed in Greene's novels. One lesson is immediately evident. Greene describes how these evils are often deliberately overlooked and even supported by large segments of the population, as well as by insidious or cowardly government officials. Thus, his novels describe in detail both the major areas in which evil emerges in contemporary life and the ways contemporary societies and individuals frequently respond and interact when encountering the many manifestations of evil. Another major theme of Part I, which is always clear to the sensitive reader of Greene's novels—albeit not necessarily to many scholars who have discussed his books—is this: Evil exists here and now, and any attempt to flee from confronting it is cowardly!

The theme of Part II is the unsung heroes who fight evil. What unites these unsung heroes? Most probably Graham Greene's belief, perhaps best expressed by Doctor Magiot, one of the unsung heroes in *The Comedians*, that the greatest mistake made by most people in twentieth-century society is their choice to be indifferent and to abandon faith in changing the world for the better. All of Greene's unsung heroes decide to rebel against this widespread and crippling indifference. They choose to fight evil. What characterizes such a decision? Who are the people who decide to fight?

Greene's novels provide important answers to both questions. Courage, sensitivity, lucidity, the willingness to see the evil in specific situations for what it is, a willingness to perceive horror and be repulsed by it, a sense of humor, a belief in the integrity of each human being, resoluteness—these decisions, attitudes, and approaches often characterize his heroes' choices to fight evil. Greene's answers, however, are not abstract formulas. They are decisions, attitudes, and approaches that emerge in real life, in concrete and often threatening situations. I suspect that, if asked, many scholars would acknowledge these attitudes and approaches to life as important. Yet, as indicated, they are rarely discussed in contemporary scholarship, except by some students of existentialism.

It is precisely the adverse situations in which many of Greene's unsung heroes fight evil that present an important insight: Quite often a person's integrity shines through his or her failure in the struggle against evil. That insight informs *The Power and the Glory*, *England Made Me*, *A Burnt-Out Case*, *The Comedians*, *The Confidential Agent*, *Stamboul Train*, and other novels. It even emerges in Greene's personal chronicle, *Getting to Know the General*. Although this insight underlies many of the following discussions, I am also stressing it at the outset because of its overwhelming importance for contemporary life. Greene's novels repeatedly show us, the simple people of the world, that, by fighting evil, even in uncomplex cases, we can often ensure our integrity! And we can do it despite the sticky, seductive mediocrity daily thrust upon us by corporate capitalist culture.

Part III focuses upon the wisdom emanating from and attained by Greene's unsung heroes. Do these simple people who fight evil attain wisdom? What constitutes their wisdom? Can we learn from these heroes about our personal lives and about the society in which we live?

Since Greene's unsung heroes often fail, they attain wisdom by learning to cope with failures while fighting evil. They also learn from their failures. Put differently, the unsung heroes are stubborn; they do not give up easily. They struggle to the bitter end. Furthermore, when they fail, they display almost no bitterness, no resentment, no hatred of the good. One finds in them none of the inane and debilitating attitudes—such as cynicism, flight from freedom, or apathy—that Friedrich Nietzsche attributed to the mediocre, cowardly herd. This ability to fight evil without resentment, to endure failure without bitterness or cynicism, to belong to society without joining the herd is what makes Greene's unsung heroes into conveyers of a wisdom rarely found in twentieth-century literature. Moreover, it is by their willingness to transcend, placidly and courageously, the failure-success syndrome, so central to bourgeois life, that the being of these unsung heroes attains a tragic dimension, albeit partially. It is interesting to note that many novelists, from Franz Kafka to Saul Bellow, have shown the inanity and insipidity that overwhelm contemporary human existence with the vanishing of the tragic dimension of life. They have not indicated, as Greene has done, that fighting evil is a way of transcending this inanity and insipidity.

The conclusion will briefly point out some of the educational, philosophical, and existential implications that arise from my discussion of Greene's unsung heroes.

≈

While writing this book, two central characteristics of Greene's novels repeatedly aroused my admiration. First, a major source of the evil that Greene's unsung heroes fight is a group of political regimes led by live politicians who share the world with us. His books describe the political evils done by leaders in contemporary Haiti, the United States, France, Mexico, the Soviet Union, England, and quite a few other countries. Consequently, his novels provide a poignant statement about the evils that currently exist in the world—evils that are frequently concealed from the public eye by the clever and mendacious rhetoric spread by the mainstream media, which usually support the government by not mentioning its evil deeds.

Through the struggles against the evil of these politicians, Greene sketches the political options open to those who fight such evil. Since fighting political evil is rarely discussed elsewhere, these options are very significant for developing a political philosophy based on freedom and the pursuit of justice. Thus, Greene's insights into evil can provide the basis for a philosophical approach that supports fighting against politically evil regimes in contemporary society. Put differently, his poignant portrayal of unsung heroes is an important contribution to political philosophy and, as such, to wisdom. Some elements of this contribution emerge in the course of this book.

Second, in his preface to *The Nigger of the Narcissus*, Joseph Conrad wrote that the art of writing is an "attempt to render the highest kind of justice to the visible universe, by bringing to light the truth, manifold and one underlying its every aspect."[3] Like Conrad, Graham Greene struggled to bring to light the truth underlying many aspects of the visible universe. He often succeeded, which makes him a great artist. He did so as a storyteller, using vivid, uncomplex, down-to-earth language. Greene seemed to sense that truth is often obscured or veiled by the uncommitted and purposely obscure language that has become fashionable in the past eighty years, especially with the increasing popularity of the behavioral and social sciences.

I wish to emphasize this point. The language of Greene's novels is clean and committed. Evil is evil is evil, much as, for Gertrude Stein, a rose is a rose is a rose. Indeed, the cleanliness of discourse and the commitment to truth and justice that repeatedly emerges in Greene's novels have made them into a verdant oasis that beckons from afar to us, weary travelers in the spiritual wasteland that capitalism continually promotes.

NOTES

1. Haim Gordon, *Quicksand: Israel, the Intifada, and the Rise of Political Evil in Democracies* (East Lansing: Michigan State University Press, 1995).

2. Two publishing houses that publish books describing the evil of contemporary regimes and, at times, ways of struggling against it are South End Press in Boston and Zed Books in London. Some books on evil, including my own, have been published by university presses or commercial publishing houses. Still, the number of scholars who address the widespread evil that Graham Greene described and which continues to exist and to ruin the freedom of large sections of humanity is exceedingly small. Some of the works of these scholars will be mentioned in the course of this book.

3. Joseph Conrad, *The Nigger of the Narcissus/ Typhoon and Other Stories* (Middlesex, England: Penguin, 1986), 11.

Part I

Evil

1
Manipulative Evil

Is there any difference between the manipulative evil of Pinkie Brown in *Brighton Rock*, that of Aunt Augusta in *Travels with my Aunt*, or that of Erik Krough in *England Made Me*? Not at all! Each character manipulates other people and willingly destroys their freedom in order to attain personal and material gains. Pinkie Brown, a small gang leader and so-called bookie-protector, murders two men and manipulates Rose, a waitress whom he despises, into marrying him so that she can refuse to give evidence that would convict him of one of the murders. Later he tries to manipulate Rose into committing suicide. Aunt Augusta, whose past as a high-class strumpet and a joyful companion of racketeers, felons, and Italian fascists who worked with the Nazis gradually emerges, easily manipulates her bored bachelor son, Henry Pulling, to join her in repeatedly breaking the law. The final pages show him willingly supporting both an Italian collaborator with the Nazis and the corrupt, oppressive, evil, dictatorial fascist regime in Paraguay. Erik Krough, the head of a multinational corporation, brutally manipulates his aides, forcefully oppresses and tricks his workers, and helps to cover up a murder, in addition to insidiously deceiving millions of investors.

Are there any differences in the spiritual hollowness of these three Greene characters? Not at all! Yet, one difference in their attempts to conceal their hollowness immediately stands out. Aunt Augusta is the most seductive of the three; she has molded her spiritual hollowness into a personal charm that assists her in seducing and manipulating people. As Greene shows, for a bored person like Henry Pulling, she is thus the most dangerous of the three. (I shall return to the curse of boredom later in this chapter.) Despite his vacuous existence and his life of ennui, Henry Pulling would probably be able to discern and reject the manipulative evil of Pinkie Brown. He might also have distanced himself from most of the evil deeds of Erik Krough. With Aunt Augusta, he is like clay in the hands of a sculptor. Make no mistake, however. Aunt Augusta's seductive and ruthless charm has nothing worthy to offer. As the book ends, one discerns the revolting, maladroit life of a smuggler and lawbreaker that she has molded for her bored son.

What is manipulative evil? Why is it so prevalent? Manipulative evil emerges when one relates to other people merely as a means to one's own evil ends. Greene shows that, when relating to the people you encounter merely as means becomes central to your existence, when you refuse to contemplate or to establish other relations with people, then, like Erik Krough, Pinkie Brown, and Aunt Augusta, you have rescinded almost all ability to share with others. Genuine reciprocity has vanished.

This point needs to be emphasized. A person who daily engages in manipulative evil knows only how to use other persons; he or she never shares with others. Greene also shows that such a person can never relate to others dialogically. Erik Krough, Aunt Augusta, and Pinkie Brown are examples of such persons, even though they come from different social levels (or classes). Of course, there are moments in which these three characters attempt to share, at least partially, with others—Aunt Augusta's stories to Henry are, at times, an example of such an attempt. But the overall orientation of these characters—what Sartre would call their life projects—is geared to always manipulating others so as to attain one's own selfish ends.

Manipulative evil can use psychological means. In A Burnt-Out Case, Greene shows how Andre Rycker uses bizarre psychological and religious methods of oppression to maneuver his young wife, Marie, who is so young that she could be his daughter, into a situation in which her freedom is destroyed. Marie rebels against the egocentric, stupid, and evil manipulations of Rycker in a subtly childish manner, which seems to be the only way that she can salvage a bit of freedom from the clutches of Rycker's uncouth religious fanaticism. She never confronts her asinine, callous husband straightforwardly; she seems to have sensed correctly that confronting Rycker would only bring an insensitive and violent response.

In his novels, Greene shows dozens of instances where manipulative evil prevails. Is he exaggerating? I think not. In the twentieth century, manipulative evil has emerged as central to both capitalist and Marxist regimes; it flourishes through the work of journalists, like Parkinson in A Burnt-Out Case, and is supported by dedication to "the system," like that of the lieutenant in The Power and the Glory or of the bishop in Monsignor Quixote. And, of course, it is part of the daily work of CIA (Central Intelligence Agency) officers like Mr. Quigly in The Captain and the Enemy and Alden Pyle in The Quiet American. In capitalist countries, manipulative evil is often hidden under the locution "pursuit of interests"—a pursuit that seemingly underlies Erik Krough's fabulous success. In Marxist countries, manipulative evil may be concealed by the phrase "fulfilling the ideals of the state," which is what the murderous lieutenant in The Power and the Glory was sure that he was doing.

Here and there, the manipulative evil of certain leaders, nations, or groups may be blocked by the struggles of persons or groups who suffer from this evil. At times, in the political realm, such struggles may lead to partial or wholesome compromises or changes for the better. Thus, the Palestinian uprising against two decades of Israeli oppression, the intifada, has led, finally, to a peace process in which Palestinians have regained some of their political and human rights.

No. Graham Greene is not exaggerating. The imaginary situations presented in his novels disclose the blunt and horrible truth about human existence in the twentieth century. Wherever you look, manipulative evil prevails; it is frequently accepted calmly and supported by our leaders, by the promoters of our political and economic systems, by mainstream journalists, by many intellectuals of all stripes, by millions of bureaucrats, and by many hundreds of millions of ordinary people. In many cases, persons who instigate terrible instances of manipulative evil are considered worthy of respect. One highly visible example is the respect awarded Richard Nixon, who was a master at performing manipulative evil. (Other U.S. presidents of the past four decades do not lag far behind him.) Indeed, as suggested again and again in Greene's novels, perhaps the most depressing characteristic of life in the twentieth century is that very often manipulative evil prevails unchallenged—it does not even arouse horror!

I have not yet fully answered the question of why manipulative evil is prevalent in the twentieth century. An immediate answer is that there are not enough persons to fight this evil. Fighters against evil are scarce. If Ida Arnold in *Brighton Rock* had not intervened, Pinkie would probably have continued his evil doings and his rampage of murders. If Thomas Fowler in *The Quiet American* had not helped the communists murder Alden Pyle, Pyle would have continued his murderous initiatives, which included the indiscriminate bombing of innocent people by what he called The Third Force. This answer is still premature, however. Moreover, it merely leads to the question: Why are there so few unsung heroes?

Manipulative evil is common and accepted in the twentieth century, Greene's novels suggest, because it flourishes "naturally" in the economic, social, cultural, and political structures that govern our life and that we support through our daily actions. In short, since Greene's novels deal primarily with the West, capitalism, especially corporate capitalism, very often nurtures manipulative evil. Why does it flourish "naturally"? One reason is that we have learned to develop certain basic existential attitudes that support these structures and encourage evil to flourish. In this chapter, I discuss three such attitudes.

One attitude is nurturing mistrust of the world. Many people become so committed to mistrusting whomever they encounter that their basic attitude toward the world is existential mistrust. Existential mistrust can be defined by the statement: If I want to exist, I must mistrust you.[1] Consider *The Power and the Glory*. A basic difference between the lieutenant and the whiskey priest is that the priest trusts the world and its inhabitants, while the lieutenant, despite his wish to bring good, continually nurtures mistrust of the world and of his fellow men and women. This nurturing is part of his existential project. Yet, Greene shows that the lieutenant seems to sense that nurturing existential mistrust is ruinous for his soul; hence, he also strives continually not to develop existential mistrust. This internal conflict contributes to the tragedy of his life.

Many of Greene's novels show a similar contrast between major characters. Ida Arnold spontaneously, resolutely, and often joyfully trusts the world and the people whom she encounters. This trust leads to her brief friendly encounter with Hale. Pinkie Brown persistently nurtures his mistrust of everyone, even faithful members of his gang. Pinkie's basic attitude toward the world is existential mistrust. The lives of Pinkie and the lieutenant reveal that there is a vicious circle here. Mistrust of the world is encouraged by the economic, social, cultural, and political structures that govern contemporary life; in turn, such mistrust supports these structures.

People who choose to nurture mistrust and to engage in manipulative evil know very well that they must conceal their basic mistrust and their wicked deeds. Erik Krough in *England Made Me* conceals his pernicious acts with the help of his great wealth, which endows him with the protective sheen of capitalist respectability; he also demands absolute loyalty from his close employees. In his relations with Rose, the eighteen-year-old Pinkie Brown plays with the supposed respectability of a man of the world so as to conceal his insidious ways of manipulating her life and affection. He demands unswerving loyalty from his gang members. Aunt Augusta likewise demands total loyalty from Henry Pulling, and she hides her evil deeds under the respectability that supposedly accrues from her age, her delightful memories, and her supposed devotion and loyalty to fellow felons and seducers. Despite these attempts at concealing their mistrust of the world, Greene shows that the mistrust of these three characters continually corrodes their being.

Someone may say that, by linking mistrust, the manipulation of other people, and counterfeit respectability, Greene is not showing much that is new. More than three centuries ago, that great thinker, Thomas Hobbes, set forth the philosophical ground rules of bourgeois life and culture when he explained:

> The finall Cause, End or Designe of men, (who naturally love Liberty and Dominion over others,) in the introduction of that restraint upon themselves, (in which wee see them live in Common-wealths,) is the foresight of their own preservation, and of a more contented live thereby; that is to say, of getting themselves out from the miserable situation of Warre, which is necessarily consequent (as hath been shewn) to the natural Passions of men, when there is no visible Power to keep them in awe, and tye them by feare of punishment to the performance of their Covenants. [sic][2]

Hobbes believed that he was simply recognizing the natural human condition of conflict. The result of this condition was quite clear; it is necessary to nurture mistrust constantly. "And Covenants, without the Sword, are but Words and of no strength to secure a man at all" [sic].[3] Indeed, the ontology of relentless conflict underlying Hobbes' political philosophy leads quite easily to mistrust of other persons and to the need always to manipulate other human beings so as to survive the constant state of war into which, supposedly, we are born. Success in such a war of survival commands respect. Thus, if Greene is merely showing that existence in our Hobbesian world requires adopting the existential attitude of nurturing mistrust, what is his contribution to understanding the prevalence of manipulative evil?

Graham Greene is no philosopher. He is not trying to argue for or against Thomas Hobbes. He is a storyteller. Still, his books show the personal and social devastation that emerges when a person nurtures mistrust of the world and its inhabitants. We learn from his novels the terrible personal and political results of living out Hobbes' bourgeois-oriented, spiritually barren philosophy. We also learn that the twentieth-century communist regimes, specifically the Soviet Union, are frequently merely a variation on the theme of Hobbesian principles. Indeed, the regimes that are manifestations of Marx's materialism live quite comfortably with Hobbesian principles.

Greene's novels do suggest three important truths that link choosing to nurture mistrust with manipulative evil. First, given the prevailing social, political, cultural, and economic structures, persons nevertheless *choose* to live in a Hobbesian world and to nurture mistrust of the world every day. Greene's novels show that, despite Hobbes' philosophy and despite the prevalence of economic, social, cultural, and political structures in which manipulative evil prevails, a person can choose to trust the world, as, for instance, the whiskey priest does. He also shows that, in rare moments, Erik Krough and Pinkie Brown are thrust into a situation where they confront the possibility of trusting a person. At that moment, in that situation, trust emerges as an opening to a new way of existing. Erik Krough and Pinkie Brown see the opening and, after a short moment of what Kierkegaard called anxiety when facing the Good, they retreat. Immediately, their well-grooved evil habits again dominate their being. They choose to continue to nurture mistrust, to manipulate other people, to destroy their own freedom and the freedom of others.

Greene is indicating that even people who have totally committed themselves to living in accordance with the "miserable situation of Warre," in which mistrust and manipulating other people are the norm, even these people can transcend a Hobbesian existence toward a more worthy life of trust, generosity, and genuine sharing. Thus, one reason for the prevalence of manipulative evil is the choices made by leaders and ordinary people to ignore the possibilities of trustful, sharing relationships that emerge in their lives. In addition, through the lives of Pinkie Brown, Erik Krough, the lieutenant, Rycker, Parkinson, and others, Greene indicates that, without relationships based on trust, people become spiritually barren.

That is the second truth. A Hobbesian world creates a spiritual wasteland, because existential mistrust of the world leads to spiritual hollowness. There is a dialectic here, because spiritually hollow people choose to live an existence that accords with Thomas Hobbes' philosophy. Greene is quite exceptional in showing the necessary linkage between spiritual hollowness and a Hobbesian world. Look again at his spiritually barren characters. What concerns Aunt Augusta, Erik Krough, Pinkie Brown, and even the Assistant Commissioner in *It's a Battlefield*? Only survival and success! Only, as Hobbes put it, "their own preservation, and of a more contented live thereby." Never anything worthy, such as truth, justice, beauty, wisdom, or love. Aunt Augusta seems to be seeking love, but her egotistical desire is a bizarre caricature of genuine love. Thus in our world, as Greene's novels correctly describe it, lawmakers, policemen, journalists, government officials, CIA officers, priests, and eminent corporate leaders join together with swindlers, racketeers, and small crooks to choose a Hobbesian existence and create a spiritual wasteland. Such choices make these people spiritually hollow and constitute them as the mortar, bricks, and pillars of a spiritually destitute Hobbesian edifice, in all its economic, social, cultural, and political manifestations.

Third, Greene's novels are written with the implicit assumption that the supporters of the Hobbesian system in which we exist are evil, brutal, bizarre, and clever. They seek and often find ways to punish severely the few exceptional, courageous fighters against both manipulative evil and widespread oppression who defy them. Unfortunately, Greene's assumption is true. Here are just a few examples of courageous fighters against evil, all of whom were severely punished by supporters of the prevailing wickedness in our Hobbesian system during Greene's long life. Rosa Luxemburg, Martin Luther King, and Archbishop Oscar Arnulfo Romero were assassinated by thugs employed by evil capitalist-oriented politicians; Che Guevara was killed by Bolivian soldiers led by U.S. rangers; Nelson Mandela sat twenty-seven years in a South African jail; and Antonio Gramsci died in an Italian jail, incarcerated by a fascist regime supported by Western capitalist countries. Note that each of these fighters was a person who had spiritual goals and a worthy spiritual message.

The media and many intellectual toadies who support the system in a Hobbesian world often help to make other exceptional fighters disappear from history. That is probably one reason that Greene wrote the chronicle *Getting to Know the General*, so as not to allow the media and pernicious Hobbesian historians to efface the just struggles of General Omar Torrijos Herrera of Panama. Unfortunately, few intellectuals struggle to save such fighters against manipulative and political evil from the attempts to efface them from history. Aleksandr Solzhenitsyn is an exception, as his three-volume masterpiece *The Gulag Archipelago*, reveals. This masterpiece describes in great detail the evil methods that Joseph Stalin used to jail, to degrade, and to kill millions of innocent human beings in the Soviet Union. With great sensitivity, the chapter "Several Individual Stories" at the end of Volume 2 of this work describes remarkable fighters against evil, who, through Stalin's methods, supported by many Soviet intellectuals, have been made to disappear from history. Solzhenitsyn wants to rescue the names and stories of these few unsung heroes, so that they will not remain in the quagmire of Stalinist oblivion.[4]

Greene's novels seldom describe such remarkable fighters against manipulative and political evil. Doctor Magiot in *The Comedians* is an exception, representing a plausible mentor for all the unsung heroes whom Greene describes. We shall return to this courageous doctor. Suffice here to say that Doctor Magiot seems to have been able to help and to encourage simple people to challenge firmly the manipulative and political evil that they daily encounter in Haiti. Yet even without Doctor Magiot, Greene is definitely indicating that we simple people, if we trust the world, can fight evildoers, and, at times, though rarely, succeed.

~

Nurturing mistrust, as an existential project, takes its toll. When mistrust is central to a person's being-in-the-world, that person must persistently desensitize himself or herself—to horror, to beauty, to the sufferings and dreams of other people, to friendship and love, to many other sensitive responses to our fellow human beings. In addition, the nurturing of mistrust murders spontaneity. The mistrustful person is always calculating. This is the second existential attitude that a person who engages in manipulative evil must adopt.

There is a vicious circle here. Engaging in manipulative evil and nurturing mistrust require desensitizing oneself and killing one's spontaneous responses. The continual desensitizing of oneself and the killing of one's spontaneity create a situation whereby other people are viewed not as partners to the world, but rather as objects to be manipulated or as threats to one's being. Such a view of fellow human beings underlies the deeds of the evil manipulator. An extreme example of such a person is Dr. Fischer in Greene's *Dr. Fischer of Geneva or The Bomb Party*.

Furthermore, Greene's novels indicate that, for a Hobbesian approach to life to prevail, it is necessary to desensitize many people. Leaders of large economic corporations, of multinational organizations, of the CIA, of political parties, and of mafia gangs know this truth intuitively. Again and again, Greene's novels show that manipulative evil prevails because many such economic and political institutions and organizations have become experts in desensitizing the people who belong to them and who work with them. The leaders of these systems and organizations know very well that desensitized people do not fight evil. In *Our Man in Havana*, Greene reveals some of the comical aspects of such desensitized people and organizations.

In most cases, however, the doings of desensitized people are far from humorous. Consider the CIA officers Alden Pyle in *The Quiet American* and Mr. Quigly in *The Captain and the Enemy*, who are as desensitized and mean as Pinkie Brown and Erik Krough, although they are presented as much more sophisticated. Pyle's acts and responses, for instance, show clearly that desensitized people are unable to comprehend the evil in the physical destruction of other human beings and the brutal abolition of their freedom, even when it stares them in the face. Pyle's profound faith in the importance of his political manipulations and in the justifications for murder that he has been taught to recite by his CIA mentors renders him unable to respond with horror to the spectacle of innocent people lying wounded and dying from the bombing that he encouraged and supported. His desensitized being allows him to remain innocent in his own mind.

Of course, when he views the devastation he has wrought, Pyle's face becomes pale. The sight of the mauled bodies and bleeding decapitated torsos resulting from the bomb disturb him. But his major concern is the mistake in communications that made the bombing unnecessary. Pyle is also very upset about the blood that has stained his shoe, which he must clean before meeting the minister. That evening, when talking with Fowler, he regards the killed and wounded Vietnamese civilians as an unfortunate mistake, a mere blunder. He will continue his manipulations.

Another seemingly sophisticated, desensitized, evil manipulator who also always seems to remain innocent, whatever falsehoods he spreads, is the journalist
Montagu Parkinson in *A Burnt-Out Case*. The lieutenant in *The Power and the
Glory* is similarly sophisticated and seemingly innocent, yet, unlike Parkinson and
Pyle, he feels that his spontaneity and sensitivity to other persons is vanishing, and
he suffers from this loss. Montagu Parkinson is already beyond such suffering. He
has sold his soul to the devil of success.

Radically desensitized people rarely contribute of themselves to the world that
they share with others. They have blocked all possibilities of perceiving, of sensing,
of seeing the Other as a partner. Genuine dialogue is never a possibility for them,
since they do not listen to the person with whom they are speaking and never relate
to the meaning which that person is attempting to convey, only to the words and
the phrases. They incorporate these words and phrases into their own quite stupid
interpretation of the world, upon which they never dare cast doubt. Since, as
Martin Buber puts it, love exists in the house of dialogue, desensitized people are
incapable of either love or true friendship. They embrace alienation as a way of life
and dedicate themselves to what Hobbes called the "foresight of their own
preservation." In the capitalist world, such foresight frequently requires relentlessly
pursuing success.

Indeed, some of these undialogical hollow people are success stories in our
Hobbesian world. They are capable of acts of daring or courage in battle, as when
Alden Pyle saves Thomas Fowler's life or when Montagu Parkinson travels to the
heart of Africa in search of a scoop. But this daring and courage never lead to
genuine dialogue, or to thinking, to self-examination, or to the pursuit of things
that are worthy in themselves, such as truth. Greene shows that the opportunities
for dialogue and thinking emerge. Fowler again and again speaks honestly, dialogically, to Pyle, trying to encourage him to emerge from his shallow, desensitized self
and his stupid perceptions of the political situation in Vietnam and of its people.
Querry in *A Burnt-Out Case* speaks honestly and straightforwardly to Parkinson,
and even forcefully demands that he rethink his own existence—to no avail. Pyle
and Parkinson remain stuck in their commitment to the vicious demands of their
calling and to the shallow rules of life that they have chosen to guide their lives
and to internalize. Their decisions require that they close themselves to the
possibility of genuine dialogue, of thinking, of relating authentically, and of
self-examination. Thus, their daring and courage do not lead to any perception of
the truth or of the horrors of the reality that meets them daily and that they help
to sustain. Need we add that these traits never lead to civil courage or personal
depth, or to wisdom, such as that of Doctor Magiot?

These points are worth repeating. Again and again in his novels, Greene shows
that desensitized people in large capitalist institutions and political systems, like
the CIA or the international news agencies, know that, in order to succeed and be
respected, they must abide by certain rules. For Alden Pyle, these rules included
saving a fellow white man in Vietnam and notifying Fowler that he loves Phuong,
Fowler's Vietnamese woman companion, before he tries to court her. Note that
Pyle's courage in battle and his abiding by strict rules help him to conceal from

himself his total lack of sensitivity to other persons and to the horror of the injustices that he initiates. Pyle is always confident that he has acted chivalrously and from the highest motives; hence, he is innocent. Such innocence, like the supposed innocence of the Assistant Commissioner in *It's a Battlefield*, which is based on a refusal to think and a dedication solely to solving problems, persistently supports all evil.

We can now add to our answer of why manipulative evil is so common. Greene's novels suggest that evil is widespread because we are surrounded by desensitized people, like Aunt Augusta, Krough, Pyle, and Parkinson, who are among the staunch supporters of the international Hobbesian regimes that currently reign. Moreover, these evildoers are considered essential and necessary to the preservation and continuity of these regimes. By exploiting and oppressing other people, by fleeing dialogue, truth, thinking, and wisdom, these evil manipulators spread their own lack of sensitivity to other human beings. Thus, a person who daily suffers from poverty, exploitation, or oppression and who encounters a widespread lack of sensitivity among the elite may quite rapidly become desensitized as well.

Yet, Pyle, Krough, Parkinson, and many desensitized people who resemble them frequently win accolades and applause in the media, even while, often cynically, they destroy the lives and freedom of other people. Think of the praise heaped on Ronald Reagan, Richard Nixon, or Henry Kissinger, to mention just a few of the West's evil political leaders. The accolades and applause awarded to such vile manipulators of their fellow human beings assure these evil, desensitized people that they are always doing what is correct. Hence, they are innocent. This is, of course, a distorted innocence, since, to borrow a phrase from Gertrude Stein, Pyle's feelings were confined to his head. The same is true of Parkinson and Krough and of the many desensitized people who resemble them.

～

The third existential attitude is the embracing of boredom. One of the most terrifying aspects of Hobbes' philosophy is that it justifies the establishment of a commonwealth that will be totally boring—without the glory of the "astonishing achievements" that led Herodotus to write *The Histories*, without the struggle for beauty, justice, love, wisdom, or anything worthy. If "The finall Cause, End or Designe of men, . . . is the foresight of their own preservation, and of a more contented live thereby [sic]," one common outcome of such a bourgeois existence is persons like Henry Pulling in *Travels with my Aunt* and the Assistant Commissioner in *It's a Battlefield*. As Greene shows, both these boring bachelors have developed such a faith in the system to which they have dedicated their lives that they fear making any moral decisions. On the first page of *It's a Battlefield*, the Assistant Commissioner has already decided that justice is not his business; he has excluded himself from the deliberations of free persons in the *polis*. Nor is justice ever the business of Henry Pulling. Small wonder that both bachelors care very little if, in that area of the world that they encounter, manipulative evil prevails.

Look closely at these bored and boring bachelors. Both are persons who have learned always to smother their passions; throughout the novels, they continue to do so. Giving freedom to the passions, after all, can threaten their survival, their comforts and satisfactions. The great joys and enhanced existence of a passionate love that Plato described in *Phaedrus* and that Leo Tolstoy portrayed, through the characters of Levin and Kitty, in *Anna Karenina* are never a possibility that these bachelors entertain; such possibilities do not even appear on the far horizon of their existence. Furthermore, both Henry Pulling and the Assistant Commissioner have no concerns or visions that transcend the small niche in the world that they have carved out for themselves through their firm dedication to the system. In that niche, they believe that they have attained a "more contented live thereby." The result is evident. They flee from their self-imposed ennui into realms that do not demand ethical or political decisions. They care very little when encountering concrete instances of evil; for instance, the Assistant Commissioner repeatedly refuses to evaluate the decisions to convict the bus driver Drover and to sentence him to death. They have learned to support quietly the evil manipulators who surround them.

On the personal level, the lives of these boring bachelors are sterile. Both lack friends or even companions with whom they can share their lives, or rather their daily plodding flight from boredom with life. Who would want to befriend such a boring person? What could a person discuss with them? What can they share? If, as Henri Bergson has suggested, our life is like a developing melody, the lives of Henry Pulling and the Assistant Commissioner, and the millions of boring people who resemble them, is like a scratched record. It revolves in one groove, endlessly repeating the few monotonous notes of a halted tune.

Graham Greene is not alone in condemning boredom as an exquisite flower of evil whose terrible fruits we daily endure. Almost a century and a half ago, Charles Baudelaire pointed out, in his famous *Fleurs du Mal* (*Flowers of Evil*) that of all the menagerie of sin, the one most damned is boredom, because it is willing to make a shambles of the earth and to swallow existence with a yawn.[5]

In addition to Henry Pulling and the Assistant Commissioner, Greene shows many concrete instances in which people who are bored with their existence participate in making a shambles of the earth and swallowing existence with a yawn. Edward Wilson and Louise Scobie in *The Heart of the Matter* are two such bored people, as are many army and police officers in the British colony in Africa described in the novel. Wilson and Louise's response to her husband's suicide at the end of the novel is a fastidious flower of evil thriving on their ennui and boredom. Another example is Mr. Surrogate in *It's a Battlefield*—a bored, conceited, cowardly, left-wing intellectual. When confronted by a concrete instance of manipulative and political evil—that is, the bus driver Drover's being convicted to die—Mr. Surrogate, to borrow a phrase from Baudelaire's *Fleurs du Mal*, reaches euphoria as if he were smoking hookah, while dreaming of gibbets for the convicted bus driver.

Make no mistake, however. Bored people may choose to be stupid when confronted with ethical or political decisions, but they are often very clever. Their stupidity inheres in their deliberately refusing to see that a worthy life begins when one leaves behind the mediocre norms and values that capitalist society, the dogmatists of the Catholic Church, or the propounders of Marxist materialism promote. Indeed, by embracing these mediocre norms and values, such bored people condemn themselves to a shallow existence. They may suffer from their stupidity, as Louise Scobie and Edward Wilson suffer or as Mr. Surrogate suffers, but they have confined themselves to a vicious circle. They embrace values and norms that sustain their stupidity, and they utilize these values to justify their cowardly existence and support their fears. In short, central to their cowardice is the fear to transcend their superficial lives.

Cleverness helps. Frequently, it provides bored people with successes within the milieu and the system that they accept without question, to which they have committed their lives. Indeed, many of these bored, stupid, clever people are today the minor and major technicians who allow the capitalist and communist systems that prevail to continue supporting instances of manipulative evil. A striking historical example of such a bored, stupid, clever, evil person in the political realm is Ronald Reagan. I shall mention just two of his evils, which have been broadly described by scholars. First, President Reagan, who was perpetually bored at committee meetings, including meetings of his own cabinet, succeeded in throwing a party for the rich of the United States, making them even richer, at the expense of the poor. Through the evil economic policies that he initiated, he created Third World enclaves in the slums of many U.S. cities. Second, Reagan financed and firmly supported the contras, who spread destruction and death among the peasants in Nicaragua. This wreaking of destruction was a manner of fighting against the "leftist," legitimately elected, Sandinista regime.

Remember, however, that Reagan was not alone. He employed hundreds of assistants—cabinet members, government officials, many aides, civil servants—who resembled him and who daily manipulated other people to attain their evil goals.[6]

～

Two more points need to be made. First, nurturing mistrust kills joy in life and genuine sharing. The lieutenant in *The Power and the Glory* suffers from this self-inflicted malady, as does Pinkie Brown. Greene's novels suggest that the opposite is also true. One good way to struggle against manipulative evil and the existential mistrust that accompanies it is by courageously expressing trust, which means genuinely sharing one's life with others and expressing joy in life. Ida Arnold in *Brighton Rock* is such a courageous, spontaneous person, whose courage and spontaneity help her in the struggle against Pinkie's evils. Another such person is Rose Cullen in *The Confidential Agent*.

Living a life of courage and spontaneity is also the way of Doctor Magiot. This wise physician knows very well that, in a world where existential mistrust and manipulative evil reign, it takes great courage to share one's existence and joy in life genuinely. I have already noted that persons like Doctor Magiot are exceptional, both in Greene's novels and in the world. Unfortunately, much more common are people like Henry Scobie in *The Heart of the Matter*, whose lack of courage to share his existence and his small joys in life with his wife, Louise, contributes to his final choice: suicide. Louise, of course, does not encourage such sharing, but that is why courage is needed.

Second, Greene repeatedly shows that evil manipulators, who nurture mistrust and desensitize themselves, are social and political parasites. Their success and power are based upon and sustained by the trust of others. They cannot exist as evil manipulators without this trust. Often the evil mistrustful person will resemble Jim Hall in *England Made Me*, who scorns such trust except in his relations with Krough. Like Pinkie Brown, Jim Hall ridicules trust, viewing it as naive or stupid. But these mistrustful persons can do evil and manipulate others to participate in or support the evil that they do only by building upon the trust of others. Thus, if Anthony Farret had not trusted him, Hall could not have murdered Anthony. Like Pinkie Brown, however, Hall does not comprehend that, despite his success in instances of manipulative evil, by nurturing mistrust and desensitizing himself, he is limiting his possible realms of interaction within the world. Such mistrustful people frequently saw down the branch upon which they sit.

∽

I have already presented elements of a major theme that is central to this book: Doing evil requires adopting and living personally destructive attitudes. This theme is not at all new. Socrates repeatedly discussed it in the agora; Plato presented it in numerous dialogues—*Gorgias* comes to mind—and forcefully argued for it again and again. Greene's novels, however, anchor this theme in contemporary life.

It is the implicit demand to adopt self-destructive attitudes, while doing evil or letting evil be done, that often repels Graham Greene's unsung heroes. They sense that manipulating others in order to attain evil goals is like a cancer. It metastasizes throughout a person's being, wreaking havoc. They also intuitively grasp that, to succeed in acts of manipulative evil, one must nurture mistrust, desensitize oneself, and often embrace boredom. They refuse to do so, and that refusal is often the beginning of their struggle against evil.

Greene's unsung heroes perceive that the opposite is also true. Those who persistently nurture mistrust, desensitize themselves, or embrace boredom will have few qualms about joining those who engage in manipulative evil. In short, the unsung heroes intuitively know that fighting evil means choosing a worthy mode of existence. This theme repeatedly emerges in chapters that follow.

NOTES

1. My educational attempts to diminish existential mistrust between Jews and Arabs in Israel give some insight into the difficulties involved in countering this existential attitude. See Haim Gordon, *Dance, Dialogue, and Despair: Existentialist Philosophy and Education for Peace in Israel* (Tuscaloosa: University of Alabama Press, 1986).

2. Thomas Hobbes, *Leviathan* (London: Everyman's Library, 1914), 87.

3. Ibid.

4. Aleksandr Solzhenitsyn, *The Gulag Archipelago*, Volume 2, trans. Thomas P. Whitney (Glasgow: Collins/Fontana, 1976), 638–654.

5. These ideas appear in the poem "To The Reader." See Charles Baudelaire, *Flowers of Evil: A Selection*, trans. Roy Campbell (New York: New Directions, 1955), 3–5.

6. Many of Ronald Reagan's evil policies and deeds have been described in detail in books by Noam Chomsky. See, for instance, Noam Chomsky, *Necessary Illusions: Thought Control in Democratic Societies* (Boston: South End Press, 1989); Noam Chomsky, *Deterring Democracy* (London: Verso, 1991).

2
Greed and Lust for Power

This chapter might have been superfluous, if I had based this book solely on the novels of Graham Greene, supplemented by my reading of newspapers. Just open any newspaper on a given day or read a few of Greene's novels, and the evil deeds stemming from greed and lust for power are evident—indeed, they are impossible to ignore. But, as mentioned in the Introduction, once you turn to much of contemporary literary scholarship and to studies of Graham Greene's novels by so-called eminent scholars, a gestalt transformation apparently takes place. Almost all of the evil that Greene articulately describes has disappeared; greed and lust for power have well nigh vanished.

This finding in relation to Graham Greene's novels was a sad revelation. In my recent book on political evil, I dealt extensively with the cowardly manner and the distorted thinking by which the existence of evil is ignored by contemporary journalists, psychologists, behavioral scientists, political scientists, and many other academics.[1] In that study, I explained at length the immorality, shallowness, and stupidity of such indifference to the many manifestations of evil that currently prevail. Unfortunately, while writing this book, it became evident that much of the scholarly writing on Graham Greene's novels, in which evil is poignantly described, deserves the same severe criticism. Here are two examples of such scholarship that especially angered me.

Graham Greene's Childless Fathers by Daphna Erdinast-Vulcan discusses seven of Greene's novels.[2] Read this short, pseudo-psychological study from first page to last, and one will not find any mention of evil, greed, or lust for power. Erdinast-Vulcan discusses *The Comedians*, which describes Haiti under François "Papa Doc" Duvalier. It is worth repeating what Greene shows in *The Comedians*: Duvalier initiated and led one of the most evil regimes in the second half of the twentieth century with the help of his murderous, brutal, greedy, power-hungry Tontons Macoute, as well as with the firm support of the United States. The terrible evil of this regime emerges from the first pages of *The Comedians* and continues through-out the book. Yet Erdinast-Vulcan mentions Papa Doc Duvalier only in passing: "The horrifying figure of Papa Doc, the tyrant who remains shut up in his palace and orchestrates the orgy of murder and brutality, *presents a daemonic inversion of the father-figure* [italics mine]."[3]

Thus, according to Erdinast-Vulcan, Papa Doc Duvalier merely has a psycho-logical role in Greene's story. His role is to present "a daemonic inversion of the father-figure." And the horror of what the real, living Papa Doc did to the Haitians—the terrible suffering they underwent at the hands of the Tontons Macoute, the greed and lust for power that Duvalier and the ruling elite embraced and that Greene forcefully describes, and the support for this greed and lust for power given to Duvalier by the United States and other Western governments—this horror, these evils, have totally disappeared. They have vanished, due to Erdinast-Vulcan's decision to flee from confronting the harsh reality that Greene describes and, instead, to deal with inane psychological thought-models. Fighting evil is not a possibility that she can imagine.

Just to make sure that the horror of what happened in Haiti under Duvalier would not be overlooked and that his book would not be considered mere fiction, Greene added a few sentences about Haiti in his dedication to the book: "Poor Haiti itself and the character of Doctor Duvalier's rule are not invented, the latter not even blackened for dramatic effect. Impossible to deepen the night. The Tontons Macoute are full of men more evil than Concasseur."[4]

Consequently, in discussing *The Comedians*, it seems that Erdinast-Vulcan has worked very hard to ignore the horrors stemming from greed and lust for power in Haiti and the dreadful sufferings that have followed. The same is true in how she relates to other areas of the world—Paraguay, Panama, Austria, Britain, Switzer-land, and other countries—where Greene describes similar evils and their terrible results. She also seems to have purposely not noticed the evil in Greene's novella *Dr. Fischer of Geneva or The Bomb Party*, which deals directly with some of the terrifying personal and social outcomes of greed and lust for power.

Make no mistake, however. My attacks on Erdinast-Vulcan and on other scholars reveal scarcely anything new. Plato already held, in *The Republic* and other dialogues, that any knowledge divorced from an attempt to comprehend the Good is bound to lead to false and rather stupid conclusions. Erdinast-Vulcan's pseudo-psychological study is merely an addition to many such shallow and foolish presentations of knowledge.

What is significant in my criticism is that it relates to Graham Greene, who is one of the few major novelists in the twentieth century who has repeatedly described and condemned, in his novels, all manifestations of evil, including greed and lust for power. Consequently, a study of Graham Greene, such as that of Erdinast-Vulcan, that purposely ignores evil is not only poor scholarship. It is also a flight from responsibility for this world, which we share and in which evils such as greed and lust for power are evident for whoever is willing to see—at least as evident as the wicked actions of, say, the officers of the CIA, Papa Doc and the Tontons Macoute, and General Stroessner of Paraguay that Greene so forcefully describes.

~

An Underground Fate: The Idiom of Romance in the Later Novels of Graham Greene by Brian Thomas is another example of flight from responsibility.[5] In his attempt to prove his weird scholarly thesis, Thomas evades all moral decisions. Even the moral decisions that Greene's heroes make, which often, as with almost all moral decisions, are made from within a complex situation—even these moral decisions vanish.

In Greene's novel *The Third Man*, Rollo Martins kills his former friend, Harry Lime, in a police manhunt for him in the sewers of post- World War II Vienna. Martins agrees to help the British police after Lime admits to heading a racket that sells false penicillin to hospitals. These sales cause, among other horrors, the deaths of hundreds of sick, innocent children. For Martins, reaching a decision to join with the British police and hunt Harry Lime so as to end his evil racket, is not easy. Greene presents some of the complexities of Martins' difficult choice.

What has Brian Thomas to say about Rollo Martins? "In betraying and killing his friend Rollo Martins ceases to be a buffoon and becomes a type of Judas; . . . he gives features to his own 'blank face' and exorcises the embodied terror of his dream."[6] Thus, the only thing that Thomas has to say about Martins' fight against evil and crime has been relegated to the realm of the psychological. Harry Lime's greed and evil deeds have disappeared, as has his guilt. The hundreds of sick children killed by Lime's greed-driven crimes are relegated to the realm of the irrelevant, since they have nothing to do with the psychological points that Brian Thomas is supposedly making. And Rollo Martin, who decides to fight for justice and against greed and the killing of children, has become "a type of Judas."

When psychology divorces itself from life, according to a Hebrew saying, it becomes penny psychology. Throughout his scholarly study, Thomas feeds the reader scoops of penny psychology. He reaches an apogee when he makes Alden Pyle in *The Quiet American* a hero and Thomas Fowler, who helps murder Pyle, into a villain. (The manipulative evil of Alden Pyle, the CIA agent, was briefly outlined in Chapter 1. It will be discussed at greater length in later chapters.) Again, Thomas uses the term Judas, this time to describe Thomas Fowler. There is no need to present Brian Thomas' foolish, distorted thinking in detail. Yet one major point should be made. Greene's unsung heroes—Rollo Martins, Thomas Fowler, the whiskey priest, Ida Arnold, Dr. Czinner, and all the others—struggle, in their own often simple ways, for the Good and against evil. They personally experience horror when they see evil or hear of evil deeds. By making these heroes into penny-psychological cases, both Daphna Erdinast-Vulcan and Brian Thomas have effaced Greene's heroes' plodding, often unsophisticated, struggle for the Good. As I have shown in detail, such an effacing of the struggle for Good by scholars who supposedly can think lends support to the evildoers in the world.[7] Hence, through their cowardly shallowness both Daphna Erdinast-Vulcan and Brian Thomas have written studies that support both the individual evildoers in the world and the evil regimes that Greene described, hated, and despised during his life.

When scholarship dedicated to Graham Greene's novels demonstrates such an ignoring of the Good and indifference to evil, as well as shallowness, penny psychology, and downright stupidity, even the most evident aspects of evil, such as greed and lust for power, need to be discussed.

∼

According to the Bible or Herodotus, greed and lust for power seem always to have been part of human history. The past few hundred years, especially since the rise of the bourgeois, however, have added an insidious new development to these evils. Greed has become legitimate as what makes the capitalist system tick; hence, success in acting greedily has very frequently become a source of supposedly legitimate political and economic power. Erik Krough in *England Made Me*, discussed in Chapter 1, is an example of this development. Such a situation creates a vicious circle, whereby greed and lust for power are further legitimized by capitalist legislators; this legitimization gives those who succeed in their greed-driven projects additional power. Yet, most greed-driven capitalists are clever. They often attempt to conceal their greed and lust for power, and the terrible results, under seemingly lofty banners such as "free enterprise," "the blessings of a market economy, " or today, "jobs for workers." They hardly ever mention their own great profits.

Unmasking the evils and the destruction of human freedom arising from the greed and lust for power of the dominant capitalist regimes is hardly a novel enterprise. It may be difficult, however, since the mainstream capitalist media and the large publishing companies owned by capitalist corporations frequently do their utmost to hinder this unmasking. Still, there are already classic examples of such unmasking. More than 150 years ago, Friedrich Engels eloquently described and articulately documented the human degradation and the horrors of widespread poverty among the English proletariat that accompanied capitalist-legitimated greed in his *The Condition of the Working Class in England*.[8] Many good, dedicated scholars have continued in the path hewed out by Engels. Their books are published at times by university or scholarly presses, but very rarely, if at all, by the mainstream, corporation-owned presses.[9] It is worth repeating that the capitalist regime has learned to conceal its greed and lust for power by an internal censoring conducted by many publishing companies and probably even by bookstores—even while these companies extoll freedom of speech and of the press.

Here is a role for courageous, sensitive, good storytellers. By telling a good story that people want to read, they can disclose and condemn much of the greed and lust for power that sustain capitalism and ruin the freedom of hundreds of millions of people around the world. Graham Greene's novels are major works that follow this route. His legacy is worthy and significant, yet he was not alone in such praiseworthy endeavors.

In a previous study, I have shown how the 1988 Nobel laureate in literature, Egyptian novelist Naguib Mahfouz, repeatedly described and condemned the greed and lust for power sanctioned and acceptable in Egyptian society.[10] Since his storytelling was great reading and his books sold in the hundreds of thousands in Arabic countries—no minor feat in a society not educated to read novels—Mahfouz was rarely attacked for repeatedly disclosing these evils. He was attacked by Arab fanatics, and, for extended periods, his articles and some of his books were banned in Saudi Arabia and other fundamentalist countries. These oppressive regimes were very angry that Mahfouz's stories and articles advocated more freedom for women, peace with Israel, and a nonliteral reading of religious texts such as the Koran. Since 1980, I have met with Mahfouz many times to discuss his novels:

> On two occasions I asked Mahfouz directly if he did not want to convey a message in his books. The first time was on one of our first meetings in 1980. He answered jokingly: "I started writing when I was six years old. Most writers say they have a message to convey and therefore they write. But I started writing before I had a message to convey, and I enjoyed it, and it has been that way ever since." The second time, a few years later, he responded more seriously. "No, my views are not what I wished to convey in my books. Still, if you ever find that the views that I express in our meetings contradict what emerges in my books, don't believe me, believe my books."[11]

Graham Greene was a great storyteller who, unlike Mahfouz, often admitted to wanting to convey a message. Furthermore, in his novels, Naguib Mahfouz described only Egypt, his own backyard, and the greed, lust for power, and other evils of that particular society. Graham Greene's backyard was the world. He described some of the terrible outcomes of the reign of greed, lust for power, and other evils in Britain in *Brighton Rock*, *It's a Battlefield*, and other novels. He also reached into several places that are off the main track and described the terrible results of these same evils that he encountered in faraway countries. How many people would have heard of the tyrannical evils of that fascist monster, General Alfredo Stroessner, who virtually owned Paraguay for decades, with continual support of the United States, if Stroessner had not been mentioned in Greene's novels *Travels with my Aunt* and *The Honorary Consul*?

Even today, few people know the extent of Stroessner's rapacious greed and ruthless lust for power, his brutal impoverishing of the Paraguayan people, and his persistent denial of their basic human rights. To point out merely the tip of this iceberg of evil, here is a vignette about Stroessner, written by Eduardo Galeano in 1980:

> Paraguay, or the little that is left of Paraguay after so much war and plunder, belongs to General Alfredo Stroessner. Every five years this veteran colleague of Somoza and Franco holds elections to confirm his power. So that people can vote, he suspends for twenty-four hours Paraguay's eternal state of siege.
>
> Stroessner believes himself invulnerable because he loves no one. The State is him. Every day, at precisely 6:00 P.M., he phones the president of the Central Bank and asks him: "*How much did we make today?*"[12] [emphasis in original.]

In his documentary account *Getting to Know the General*, Greene describes his friendship with General Omar Torrijos Herrera, the leader of Panama. The book relates the incident of Greene's being shunned by one of General Stroessner's ministers. It occurred when Greene and the Paraguayan minister both attended the spectacular signing of the Panama Canal Treaty by General Omar Torrijos Herrera and U.S. President Jimmy Carter in Washington, D.C., in 1977. Carter invited General Stroessner to be a guest of honor at this signing; Greene accompanied General Torrijos. The only reason for Greene's being shunned by the Paraguayan minister was the descriptions of the evil regime in Paraguay in his novels.

I discuss political evil in the next chapter, yet it is worthwhile here to look again at the fact that General Stroessner was a guest of honor at the signing, invited by President Carter. This invitation confirms the explicit support that General Stroessner continually received from President Carter, who liked to impress the media in the world as being sincerely concerned that human rights not be abused. In reality, President Carter continued the policy of all the presidents of the United States who firmly supported and gave aid to all the evil dictators in Central and South America—dictators who brutally oppressed and exploited the population of their countries and totally disregarded their human rights. Greene's novels repeatedly reveal the firm support, and often the direct orders, that greedy, power-hungry dictators, such as Stroessner, received from the United States and other Western powers.

Much is disclosed of U.S. support for the evil regimes and for greedy dictators in Paraguay and Argentina in *The Honorary Consul* and *Travels with my Aunt*. In addition, the remarkable Doctor Magiot in *The Comedians* is murdered by Papa Doc Duvalier so as to appease and satisfy the U.S. government. The U.S. government has instigated and perpetrated many evils and horrors, directly or clandestinely through the CIA and other organizations, on behalf of power-lustful and greedy dictators in Chile, Guatemala, Nicaragua, Vietnam, the Philippines, Panama, and many other places in the world in which corporate capitalists based in the United States rapaciously exploit the indigenous population. Anyone who has followed these events even partially will not be surprised when he reads Greene's novels. For others, these evils may be a revelation, and Greene deserves full credit for revealing and condemning both this evil and the specific evildoers. Although these wicked deeds are often in the background of Greene's stories, one cannot help perceiving that Greene has depicted the evils performed by the U.S. government and by other Western powers during most of the twentieth century accurately. Greene also makes it clear that lust for power and greed are the driving forces behind many of these evils.

~

Greed and lust for power bring many additional evils in their wake. Greene presents quite a few of these evils clearly. So as to silence criticism of General Stroessner, Edward Plarr's father, in *The Honorary Consul*, is jailed, cruelly tortured, and finally killed by the Paraguayan police in an escape attempt. Greene lucidly shows that the rampant abuse of human rights in Paraguay is a clear outcome of Stroessner's unbridled greed and lust for power, which is supported by Western capitalist regimes whose multinational corporations bleed the country. Greene also discloses that, since greedy people are frequently clever and crafty, they often trap honest people in their web. The relentless greed of the Syrian trader, Yusef, in *The*

Heart of the Matter, contributes much to the downfall of Henry Scobie, who is definitely not greedy.

An important point that Greene discloses in *The Heart of the Matter* is that Yusef is attracted to the integrity of Scobie; he seems to feel his own spiritual vacuity, which is an inevitable outcome of his lifelong dedication to nurturing and pursuing his greed. Yusef seeks Scobie's friendship in order somehow to fill this vacuum. Other great authors, from Joseph Conrad to William Faulkner, have shown that, when greed and lust for power reign unchallenged, one major result, beyond the profound and lengthy suffering of the oppressed, is the spread of spiritual vacuity. One significant outcome of the flourishing of capitalism, which legitimize greed and lust for power (much as President Jimmy Carter legitimized General Stroessner at the signing of the Panama Canal Treaty), is that spiritual vacuity becomes acceptable. Few dare to criticize it. In many of his novels, Graham Greene vividly describes this vacuity and portrays the human degradation that it entails.

What do I mean by spiritual vacuity? In Faulkner's novels, spiritual vacuity is probably best epitomized in the personality of Flem Snopes, a major figure in the three novels usually called *The Snopes Trilogy.* The three novels describe the rise of Flem Snopes from sharecropper to bank president in Jefferson, Mississippi. Snopes' slow ascent is by base, uncanny, crafty, insidious, wicked, and yet legitimate means. It is evident that Flem Snopes has chosen the satisfaction of greed and lust for power as his life project. The results are sad and ominous. Snopes cannot establish meaningful relations with any person, nor can he relate to anything worthy. He cannot discuss a topic that has not to do with business. He is hollow, boring, physically and spiritually impotent—and evil. Flem Snopes' unprecedented success reveals the triumph of today's ruthless capitalism over the remnants of what was considered Southern gentry. Put bluntly, it is the victory of unmasked greed and lust for power over the decadent Southern gentleman's existence that Faulkner describes as prevailing in his mythical Yoknapatawpha County.[13]

In contemporary capitalist society, Flem Snopes is a bit of an exception, in that he never dons the mask of sophistication or inherent respect. His greed and lust for power are as evident, to whoever cares to look, as his white shirt and short black tie. Greene's novels are much more realistic, in that he shows how greed and lust for power are disguised, as is the spiritual vacuity that accompanies them. Erik Krough, the head of a transnational corporation in *England Made Me,* also chooses the satisfaction of greed and lust for power as his life project. He is as spiritually vacuous as Flem Snopes. Like Snopes, he cannot establish meaningful relations with any person, nor relate to anything worthy. He cannot intelligently discuss a topic that is not about business. But he conceals both his greed and lust for power under the mask of sophistication. He orders a fountain by a famous contemporary Swedish sculptor as a centerpiece for the building that houses his headquarters, yet he cannot relate to the fountain. He goes to the opera and falls asleep in one of the best seats in the orchestra section; to make sure that nobody notices his drowsiness, he purchases all the seats around him and leaves them vacant. At a meeting at the British embassy in Stockholm, where they are celebrating a new book of poems by the minister, Krough flips through the book and reluctantly admits that he does not understand poetry. Even though Krough's mask of sophistication often slips from his being, disclosing his spiritual vacuity, the people surrounding him duly ignore it. Thanks to his wealth, he is invited to major social events: he is respected, admired, followed by reporters, and often consulted on financial matters by those with whom he socializes.

The concealment of this spiritual vacuity and the adoption of a counterfeit sophistication is straightforwardly condemned in *Dr. Fischer of Geneva or The Bomb Party*. This novella has much black humor that describes the depths to which greed can lead so-called respectable people. By playing lewd, sordid games that humiliate his guests, Dr. Fischer seemingly helps them to legitimize their insatiable greed. But such a playing of games is merely another manner of unmasking the counterfeit sophistication of greed-driven people and of exposing the spiritual vacuity that must accompany a life dedicated to greed. When he succeeds in totally unmasking the cowardly avarice of his guests, when, at the bomb party, Dr. Fischer succeeds in exhibiting their baseness for what it is, nothing is left for Dr. Fischer except despair and suicide. Note that Dr. Fischer's inability to establish reciprocal friendly relations with anybody is evident.

Spiritual vacuity also characterizes the CIA agents whom Greene describes, including Alden Pyle in *The Quiet American*, Tooley in *Travels with my Aunt*, and Mr. Quigly in *The Captain and the Enemy*. Their role is supposedly to protect the interests of the U.S. government, as well as the values of democracy and of the so-called free world. They all embrace the ideology of the institutions that enlisted them, to protect and support the seemingly worthy tenets and principles of democracy in the United States. But, as Greene shows, in real life, that means to protect the interests of the large corporations based in the United States whose greed and lust for power have created the neocolonialism that wreaks devastation upon hundreds of millions of impoverished and exploited people in the Third World. Much as these agents of neo-colonialism endeavor to conceal their pernicious role and evil deeds, Greene makes sure that their daily evils emerge in his novels. He also shows that the ideological principles that supposedly guide these agents of the West are merely self-serving ruses of large financial conglomerates and of other Western powers.

Mr. Quigly is a secondary figure, appearing only toward the end of the story. His evil is disclosed, his indifference to justice and to human suffering is perceived, and his ruthlessness is evident, but his spiritual vacuity is only partially glimpsed. Like bad breath, it accompanies his speech and deeds. Tooley, on the other hand, suffers a bit from the spiritual vacuity that accompanies his work and daily deeds. He is divorced and lonely, has no inkling what is happening with his only daughter, and has no worthy relationship with her. Despite a few moments of personal anxiety about his life, Tooley has no qualms about his evil undertakings, which include making a deal with a former Nazi collaborator. He also lives amiably with smugglers and other lawbreakers in Paraguay, often lending them support. He never questions whether such deeds contradict the ideology of freedom or democracy to which the CIA is supposedly committed. The only serious endeavor he can undertake, outside of his constant dedication to his work, is counting the seconds each day he spends urinating and faithfully recording this finding in a small notebook, for the use of future research.

Alden Pyle's spiritual vacuity has been described partially in Chapter 1; it is a sophisticated vacuity that differs somewhat from that of Krough, Tooley, or Quigly. Like Krough, Pyle has no sensitivity to other people, neither to Fowler nor to the Vietnamese, nor even to Phuong whom he professes to love. He is committed to the ideology of the West and never dares question it, even when he is in personal danger from the Vietnamese and spends the evening at a lookout post discussing some aspects of this ideology with Fowler. Furthermore, he is delighted that the deeds needed to support this ideology have been spelled out in a book by York Harding.

As already indicated, without sensitivity to other people, one can hardly relate spiritually. But with Pyle, who is younger than Krough, opportunities for change appear and challenge him. Again and again, Fowler tries to explain himself and his views of the situation to Pyle, but these explanations never penetrate further than the surface of Pyle's understanding. Pyle does not allow them to break through the shell of his inane ideological commitment to the policies of the United States and to the suggestions formulated by York Harding. It is worth repeating that even the squirming, decapitated torsos of Vietnamese civilians, which have resulted from a mistaken bombing that he has initiated, do not challenge Pyle to reevaluate his life and commitments. For Pyle, the Vietnamese, except Phuong perhaps, are no more than puppets in a show that he is codirecting; Fowler is a fellow white man who should be respected but never listened to carefully.

~

Now we can formulate a major theme that appears in many of Greene's writings. Spiritual vacuity begins when individuals have trained themselves never to listen carefully to fellow human beings, not to see the evils encountered in the world, and to refuse to think. This is a training that is encouraged by the large corporations that rule much of the economy and by many political leaders. Need we add that the covert and other representatives of U.S. greed and lust for power—the CIA agents, many career diplomats and army officers—are trained to be spiritually vacuous. They learn to accept without question the prevailing ideology and its conclusions, never to listen to human beings, except their superiors or peers, not to see evils that they encounter and in which they may participate, and not to think. How? By learning always to be indifferent to human suffering, to oppression, to exploitation, and to other crimes that result from the deeds of their greedy and powerful employers.

How does a person learn to be always indifferent to greed, lust for power, and other evident evils? One of Greene's poignant answers is by abandoning all faith in the possibility of establishing a better world, in which freedom, justice, dialogue, respect for all human beings, and authentic sharing will reign. In order not to be indifferent, you must not abandon faith, Greene holds. Listen to Doctor Magiot's legacy in his parting letter to Brown in the final pages of *The Comedians*: "I implore you—a knock on the door may not allow me to finish this sentence, so take it as the last request of a dying man—if you have abandoned one faith, do not abandon all faith. There is always an alternative to the faith we lose."[14]

Later in this study I shall return to the terrible outcomes of indifference and to the importance of embracing and attempting to realize a faith in a better world.

NOTES

1. Haim Gordon, *Quicksand: Israel, the Intifada, and the Rise of Political Evil in Democracies* (East Lansing: Michigan State University Press, 1995).

2. Daphna Erdinast-Vulcan, *Graham Greene's Childless Fathers* (London: Macmillan, 1988).

3. Ibid., 82.

4. Graham Greene, *The Comedians* (London: Penguin, 1967), 5–6.

5. Brian Thomas, *An Underground Fate: The Idiom of Romance in the Later Novels of Graham Greene* (Athens: University of Georgia Press, 1988).

6. Ibid., 11.

7. Gordon, *Quicksand*.

8. Friedrich Engels, *The Condition of the Working Class in England* (Middlesex, England: Penguin, 1987). This study was first published in Germany in 1845.

9. Small committed presses will often publish scholarly works on the evils of capitalism. Examples are South End Press in the United States and Zed Books in Britain.

10. Haim Gordon, *Naguib Mahfouz's Egypt: Existential Themes in His Writings*. (Westport, CT: Greenwood, 1990).

11. Ibid., 2.

12. Eduardo Galeano, *Memory of Fire*. Part III: *Century of the Wind*, trans. Cedric Belfrage (New York: Pantheon, 1988), 258.

13. William Faulkner, *The Hamlet* (New York: Vintage, 1991); William Faulkner, *The Town* (New York: Vintage, 1961); William Faulkner, *The Mansion* (New York: Vintage, 1955). Faulkner originally published the first two volumes in the early 1930s and the last volume twenty years later.

14. Greene, *The Comedians*, 286.

3
Political Evil

Many twentieth-century novelists shy away from describing political evil, especially the political evil that currently prevails. By political evil I mean the purposeful destruction of human freedom by the rulers and agents of a political regime or by persons who wish to further their political goals. Some of the reasons that instances of political evil are not described seem evident. Powerful people in the regime that performs and supports the political evil will be indignant if an author brands it or them as evil. They may do everything in their power to limit that author's publications. That may be the reason that Joseph Conrad never mentioned Belgium or the Belgian Congo in *Heart of Darkness*. Conrad was purposely vague as to the location of the horrors that the Europeans in his novel inflicted upon Africans, horrors that he poignantly described. That may be the reason that Saul Bellow, in *Humboldt's Gift* and in other novels, describes the sordid outcomes of capitalism and of the anti-intellectualism prevailing in the United States without condemning the political evil of the regime straightforwardly.

Graham Greene never seems to be troubled by such considerations. In *The Quiet American*, he has no qualms when indicating that the politicians and state agencies in Washington and Paris are the major destroyers of the freedom of the Vietnamese people. These politicians have decided upon the brutal aggression of the French Army in Vietnam and have relentlessly sought ways to continue to dominate the Vietnamese people. The quiet American, Alden Pyle, is, in his own eyes, merely an innocent employee of the CIA, who has no inkling of the evil decisions of his government.

Note that *The Quiet American* was written before the United States initiated its ferocious war in Vietnam, in which it wreaked a destruction unprecedented in its horror in much of Indochina. For instance, the United States Air Force performed saturation bombings of large areas with napalm, fragmentation bombs, and other explosives that destroy nature and humans on a broad scale. This indiscriminate bombing murdered and mauled millions of innocent Vietnamese, Cambodians, and others. It also created tremendous tracts of land that resemble a moonscape. Greene seems to have had lucid insight into such possible historical developments. Through the wicked deeds of the "innocent" Alden Pyle, Greene reveals the intentions of the U.S. policymakers to dominate all of Indochina by force. In previous chapters, I have already pointed out Greene's strong condemnation of the political evil of the leaders in Paraguay and Haiti, who were also supported by the government of the United States.

Greene seems to have sensed that condemning political evil is very important, because this evil is so often concealed from the public eye by the leaders who perform it, as well as by their many toadies and supporters, including intellectuals. In a series of profound and well-documented studies, Noam Chomsky has shown that the mainstream media in the United States has always supported the political evil of the government, as long as this evil serves the interests of the capitalist elite and the major U.S.-based corporations.

Consider, for instance, the history of the past half-century in Central America and the Caribbean, areas about which Greene wrote. This period has been characterized by continual political evil, supported, initiated, and performed by the United States. Tens of millions of people in this area have undergone hunger, brutal torture, slave labor, and murder by death squads and, at times, by U.S. soldiers. Chomsky has shown that this evil derives primarily from the policies of the United States, which very often set up and always actively supported the fascist and totalitarian regimes that ruled in Guatemala, El Salvador, Honduras, Haiti, Cuba, Grenada, and other countries of the area. The United States always gave these evil regimes arms and often trained their soldiers. Policymakers in the administration and Congress rarely blinked when these soldiers conducted brutalities so as to terrorize the population into submission to the U.S. corporations that bled the countries' economic assets and exploited the populations. Yet, as Chomsky has shown, these terrible evils have been continually and consistently hidden from the U.S. public by the obedient mainstream media, led by the *New York Times* and the *Washington Post*.[1] What is more, during the past half-century, no major or celebrated novelist in the United States has written a novel describing and detailing these ongoing evils. Graham Greene did.

∼

From interviews that Greene gave and from his political writings in the press, it is evident that Greene's approach to condemning political evil is quite close to that of Chomsky.[2] As already indicated in previous chapters, this fact is often overlooked—even by people sympathetic to Greene, such as those who have written critical appraisals of his work. Here are two additional examples.

In his book *Graham Greene*, Richard Kelly has surveyed all of Greene's work without mentioning political evil. Blending what I have termed penny psychology with shallow political and social perceptions, Kelly reaches inane conclusions that totally exclude the possibility of struggling against evil from the realm of human possibilities. Indeed, fighting evil, or specifically political evil, seems to be far beyond Kelly's horizons. Thus, for Kelly, Ida in *Brighton Rock* "brings death and misery," and Alden Pyle in *The Quiet American* is merely someone carried away by "impersonal idealism." Such dense views are hardly surprising. Since Kelly refuses to see that evil and political evil exist, either in the world or in Greene's novels, he has no choice but to view Greene's characters through his shallow, distorted psychological prism.[3]

Mario Cuoto has also written a superficial book on Greene's novels, in which he evades seeing much of the evil, especially the political evil, that Greene's novels forcefully portray. This evasion is all the more surprising since, in an interview with Greene that Cuoto has included in his book, Greene firmly condemns the U.S. intervention in Vietnam and says clearly "my sympathies were and are with Vietnam."[4] Cuoto has also learned very little from Greene's letters to *The Times* of London that are included in his book. Consider a short citation from Greene's letter of January 6, 1973, in which he condemns the U.S. policy in Vietnam: "I abhor the Czechoslovak invasion . . . but I doubt if it can compare in horror and immorality with the indiscriminate bombing by napalm and fragmentation bombs of South and North Vietnam, not to speak of the only publicised massacre of women and children in My Lai."[5]

Despite the myopia of scholars who deal with Greene's writings, it is evident that Greene saw and described many of the horrors of political evil in the twentieth century. Indeed, beginning with his novels written in the 1930s, such as *Stamboul Train* and *A Gun for Sale*, for half a century Greene articulately described the political evil of existing fascist, communist, and supposedly democratic governments, as well as of the leaders of the so-called capitalist elite and the heads of transnational corporations. He also indicated that the fascist governments in non-Western countries and the major capitalist corporations are almost always firmly supported by the governments of so-called democracies. By always describing the political evil that prevails and by pointing out who supports this evil and how, Greene's novels are a major truthful testimony about much of the sordid history of the twentieth century. This testimony is very important because, as mentioned, the facts of political evil are frequently ignored by the mainstream media and by hosts of obedient scholars.

For instance, there is no question that *The Comedians* describes the truth about the horrors of U.S.-supported political evil in Haiti during the reign of Papa Doc Duvalier. Consider just three sentences from a scathing letter on American-supported oppression and exploitation of the population that led to the denial of basic human rights and the terrible poverty in Haiti. Greene wrote this letter to the editor of *Commonweal*; it was published on June 24, 1966: "It was American military aid which armed the Tontons Macoute under the old excuse that it was defending the 'free' world against Communism. (I doubt whether there were fifty Communists in Haiti.) Not all the perfumes of Arabia are going to wash out that little stain."[6]

The findings of human rights organizations fully support Greene's comments and his descriptions of corruption, oppression, and brutality in *The Comedians*. Yet Papa Doc Duvalier's brutal political evil, which human rights organizations repeatedly condemned in their publications, was almost never considered worthy of reporting by the correspondents and the editors of the mainstream media in the United States. The same is pretty much true of the media in other Western countries. Put succinctly, very often Greene's fiction is much closer to the truth than the so-called facts presented by the often deceitful mainstream media in Western capitalist democracies.[7]

～

To this point, I have mentioned quite a few scholarly works on Graham Greene, all of them unfavorably. My major reason for rejecting all these studies is that the writers have brutally divorced Graham Greene's novels from the world that they describe. I wish to emphasize this point. Graham Greene wrote about our world and its horrors, including its widespread political evil. In contrast, the scholars mentioned write with total indifference to the terrible evils and particular horrors that Greene describes and that continue to exist in our world. It is this indifference to evil, especially to political evil, that enrages me. It also frequently makes their presentations of Greene's writings asinine.

Furthermore, these scholars have done their best to ignore certain simple truths that Greene's novels frequently convey. I blush at the need to repeat these simple truths, but perhaps, once in this book, they need to be stated straightforwardly.

Whether we like it or not, this world includes much evil, including political evil. As participants in this world, we are responsible for evil's continuation if we make no attempt to stop it. Let me state this idea again. If we do nothing to halt the evil that exists, if you and I refuse to see it and to condemn it, we are fleeing our responsibility and our freedom, which are the birthrights of our humanity. As Heng says to Fowler in *The Quiet American*, "Sooner or later one has to take sides. If one is to remain human."[8]

As Greene repeatedly shows and as those willing to perceive lucidly see, most people flee the responsibility to see and to fight evil. Such a cowardly flight from responsibility characterizes all the scholarly works on Graham Greene that I have mentioned and have encountered. In addition, these works persistently exclude the fact that Greene's novels express a resounding call for responsibly stopping the evil in the world, which is why his works continually criticize indifference. Scholars writing about Greene's novels also ignore the fact that what distinguishes his unsung heroes, like Ida, Fowler, Brown, or Doctor Magiot, is their emerging from indifference and their willingness to get involved in the fight against evil here and now.

A work of scholarship on Greene's novels that ignores the political evil that Greene articulately describes, an evil that one need only open a newspaper to discover, condemns itself to banality. Indeed, banality of scholarship in relation to Greene's novels can be defined, much as Hannah Arendt defined Adolf Eichmann's banality of evil, as the refusal to see or think about the political evil staring you in the face. It is a sad testimony to the level of scholarship currently prevailing that many scholars produce such works of banality.

～

It is possible to ask: Why is the description of political evil important in a novel? Fully answering this question would require a separate study. Here I can provide only a partial answer. One major reason that the description of political evil is important is that it gives the historical setting and the characters of a novel an additional important dimension. What is that dimension? Consider the opening sentences of Aristotle's *Politics*:

> Every state is a community of some kind, and every community is established with a view to some good; for mankind always act in order to obtain that which they think good. But, if all communities aim at some good, the state or political community, which is the highest of all, and which embraces all the rest, aims at good in a greater degree than any other, and at the highest good.[9]

According to Aristotle, two components of this highest good are justice and excellence. Like Plato and other Greek thinkers, Aristotle believed that these two components, and especially justice, are unique to the political community. From Graham Greene's numerous letters to editors, from his numerous statements on injustice, and from his novels, it is clear that he accepted the assumptions of Aristotle. One can say without hesitation that Greene repeatedly demanded of all political communities with which he came in contact that they pursue the highest good. He never lowered his standards.

It is therefore evident that an author who describes political evil is adding the dimension of injustice and justice, and of the highest good attainable in politics, to the characters and to the milieu described in the novel. There are great novels in which justice and excellence are pretty much ignored. James Joyce's *Ulysses* comes to mind. Yet, very often, the ignoring of justice and of political evil in a novel leads to a vapid presentation of the period and the milieu. It seems that Tolstoy sensed this problem in *Anna Karenina*. In the last pages of the novel, he articulately describes the jejune jingoism adopted by many Russians during the Crimean war. The vacuous, often inane response of Vronsky, Oblonsky, and many other characters to this war gives a final touch to Tolstoy's condemnation of their hollow way of life, of their spiritual bankruptcy, and of the many other evils in Russian society and its aristocracy.

Political evil not only destroys the basis of justice; it often blocks the emergence of excellence, of a new beginning. This blocking of excellence rarely concerns the wicked leaders who engage in political evil, be it the Biblical Ahab, Margaret Thatcher, or Ronald Reagan. By showing the destruction of the possibility of excellence emerging, in Paraguay, Haiti, England, and other countries, Greene reveals the terrible outcomes of the political evil that prevails.

As a corollary, his novels also show that the pursuit of justice and the good can instruct the way of life of simple people. Indeed, Greene's novels are educational, since they show readers that it is possible, even for those who are not the salt of the earth, to transcend the spiritual poverty that results from political evil. This transcending frequently requires that people have the courage to fight political evil. Again, Greene's novels agree with Aristotle's *Politics*, which held that courage is crucial for the pursuit of excellence and justice. As mentioned, Greene has been a lonely voice in showing the daily difficulties of such a struggle in the evil-ridden political milieu of the twentieth century.

$\sim$

Some may say that Greene was not alone in condemning political evil. The political evil of General Franco seems to have angered Ernest Hemingway, for when he wrote *For Whom the Bell Tolls*, he forcefully condemned the wicked deeds of Franco and his fascist forces in Spain. Furthermore, it is possible to argue that in his presentation, Hemingway was appealing to his readers to join in the fight against fascism. After all, the very title comes from a John Donne sonnet that ends with the phrase: "And therefore never send to know for whom the *bell* tolls; It tolls for *thee*." And what of Heinrich Böll's attacks on the insidious evil that prevails in German society, or of Nadine Gordimer's descriptions of many manifestations of evil in South Africa?[10]

Of course, many authors have related to the widespread political evil that has prevailed in the twentieth century. Yet, it would be hard to find an author who can compare with Greene in describing in detail the breadth and depth of political evil in our century. I know of no other novelist who has depicted political evil in as many areas of the world: Vietnam, Mexico, Panama, Paraguay, England, Sweden, South Africa, Haiti, Yugoslavia, Spain—to mention some of the sites that Greene chose for his novels. Greene's work also repeatedly shows that a major source of much of the political evil that is performed can be traced to the so-called leaders of the free world: the United States, United Kingdom, and France.

What is more, Greene goes further than others in articulately portraying the depth of political evil that prevails in a Western democracy. He does so by showing the deeds, the methods, and the philosophy of the Secret Service, which is one institution that supports and constantly engages in performing political evils. *The Human Factor* is Greene's subtle yet forceful condemnation of the evils of this institution.

It is evident that a secret service agency is set up to spy on a state's external and internal enemies and to counter the espionage and the destructive deeds of those enemies. Secret institutions, however, attain a life and a morality of their own. In *The Human Factor*, Greene exposes the cynical willingness of high officers in the British Secret Service to murder innocent people and to inflict suffering upon those who do not deserve it.

A leak is traced to a small section of the Secret Service in the department headed by Sir John Hargreaves. The officers who work in that section are Maurice Castle and Arthur Davis. The leak is first discussed during a weekend evening meeting at Hargreaves' country estate after a day of pheasant hunting. The security officer, Colonel Daintry, is told by Hargreaves and his confidant and assistant, the physician, Doctor Percival, to find the source of the leak; they will take care of it. One needs little perspicuity to discover Percival's and Hargreaves' cynicism and their willingness to act illegally and do evil. They say straightforwardly that they are willing to eliminate the source of the leak quietly so as to evade questions in Parliament or any other public scandal. They are blunt and hardly attempt to conceal their wicked and illegal approach; this seems to be justified because the entire discussion is based on *realpolitik* and because the atmosphere exudes an aroma of good English manners. Indeed, Greene shows that Hargreaves' and Percival's attitude gives their political evil an aura of respectability.

Colonel Daintry feels uncomfortable; he does not like reaching major decisions without evidence; nor does he like performing and covering up acts that are illegal. He haltingly expresses reservations. When Daintry turns in to spend the night in one of the Hargreaves guest rooms, Doctor Percival enters and tries to calm him. Percival points to a Ben Nicholson painting hanging in the room and suggests that harmony in the painting is achieved by each square not interfering with the others. He tells Daintry to stay within his own yellow square and not to worry about what happens elsewhere, in other squares in the Secret Service. Thus, harmony will flourish.

It is important to emphasize that Percival's argument and general approach is what allows the widespread evil done by institutions and by political regimes to flourish. Each bureaucrat or officer in the institution remains in his or her box, not interfering with what occurs in other boxes. In this manner, the bureaucrat or officer is also covered. If scandal does erupt, he or she has never ventured beyond the boundaries of the box. I have pointed out the spiritual poverty of such an approach when discussing the way of life of the Assistant Commissioner in *It's a Battlefield*. Here I will emphasize its being the ground upon which various sorts of cynical betrayal of all principles of justice can be nurtured.

Daintry listens to Percival's argument; he hesitates but finally complies. He is especially perturbed since the idea of acting illegally and on the basis of very few facts has come from Sir John Hargreaves. Additional paltry evidence that indicates that Davis may be the source of the leak is gathered. Hargreaves gives Percival the authorization to do what need be done. While acting as Davis' medical doctor, Percival poisons him with a newly developed poison. Davis turns out to be the wrong man.

The depth of Percival's cynicism and political evil becomes evident when we recognize that he is not only performing an act of political evil. He is betraying his calling as a medical doctor. He has taken the Hippocratic oath, betrayed it, and, in the process, defiled the medical profession. Davis is Percival's patient, and Percival uses the trust a patient intuitively gives to a physician to poison him. Such a cynical betrayal of his vocation is also true of Sir John Hargreaves, who has been appointed by the government of a democracy to protect that democracy and the freedom of its people against totalitarian enemies. In the case of Davis, Sir John Hargreaves betrays and defiles the basic democratic principle that a person is innocent until proven guilty in a court of law. He agrees to have Davis murdered with almost no qualms. Indeed, Hargreaves is willing to betray all the basic laws and legal procedures of British democracy in order to avoid a publicly exposed scandal in the institution that he heads, which will be followed by questions in Parliament about his work. Moreover, the fact that he participates in deceit and murder hardly concerns him; what does concern him is keeping everything that occurs in his department hidden from Parliament and from the British public.

Greene is here pointing to a fact that emerges for anyone who wishes to look carefully at what occurs in many democracies. Members of the secret service, of the armed forces, and of the police, as well as quite a few politicians—in short, those who are employed to guard and protect human freedom—are very often betrayers of their most basic trust. They conceal this betrayal under a cover of ensuring order or of guarding the regime against so-called external or internal enemies. As Greene's novels suggest, however, the truth is that these embracers of respectability and secrecy are concerned only about their own careers and their success, which are only partially linked to the success of the institutions in which they serve. Hence, these so-called public servants could not care less about betraying the trust the public has given them and performing terrible evils. Furthermore, as indicated, very often these so-called guardians of democracy and freedom have become totally desensitized to the evils they perpetrate. Both in *The Quiet American* and in *The Human Factor*, Greene shows forcefully that performers of political evil have lost all sensitivity to the sufferings, the feelings, or the dreams of their fellow human beings, even those with whom they work. Dr. Percival's last meeting with Sarah, Maurice Castle's wife, reeks of such insensitivity.

In all fairness, Greene indicates in *The Human Factor* that the British Secret Service is not alone in being a breeding ground for political evil. A similar cynicism and willingness to do evil exists within the secret service agencies of West Germany, the Soviet Union, and South Africa, as well as in the American CIA. He thus suggests that there is little difference between the secret service of a totalitarian regime and that of a so-called democracy. Justice is never a concern of the agents or officers in these secret services. Their only wish is to succeed in outsmarting the enemy. Those ends justify any and all means. In a word, they are committed Machiavellians. This commitment means that members of a secret service agency never view other persons as genuine partners, only as objects to be manipulated. What they most fear is scandal or unexplainable failure. These fears provide much of the comic effect of *Our Man in Havana*, Greene's delightful farce about the British Secret Service.

~

To indicate briefly that Greene's novels disclose basic truths, here is one of many examples of political evil in democracies, in which the principles of democracy are betrayed by its so-called guardians. In 1946, the United States established the School of the Americas (SOA) in Panama, with the supposed mandate, as stated by the Pentagon, "to professionalize militaries in Latin America, promote democracy, and teach human rights." When the school moved to Fort Benning, Georgia, in 1984, the Panamanian newspaper *La Prensa* called it "The School of Assassins."

Evidently, *La Prensa* knew very well what it was writing. Roy Bourgeois, a Maryknoll priest who founded an organization called School of Americas Watch, has pointed out that "Consistently, Latin American nations with the worst human rights records have sent the most soldiers to the School of the Americas."[11] Looking at El Salvador's record, Bougeois has pointed out:

When the UN Truth Commission Report on El Salvador was released last year [1993], School of Americas graduates featured prominently among the perpetrators of atrocities and human rights abuses.

- Romero Assassination. 3 officers cited, 2 are SOA graduates.
- Rape and murder of 4 U.S. churchwomen. 5 Officers cited, 3 are SOA graduates.
- El Mozote Massacre. 12 officers cited. 10 are SOA graduates.
- Massacre of 6 Jesuits, their housekeeper and daughter. 27 officers cited, 19 are SOA graduates.[12]

Bourgeois has shown that these numbers are representative of much of the political evil performed in all of Latin America. Hence, for anyone who cares to look, it is evident that the School of the Americas is a training school for dictators, thugs, murderers, rapists, and death squad leaders in Central and South America. All the teachers in that school are betraying their public mandate, which,—let me cite it again—according to the Pentagon, is to promote democracy and protect human rights.

From Bourgeois' essay, one learns that the betrayal of democracy in relation to the School of the Americas reaches far beyond the administration and faculty of the school. It exists at the highest level of political institutions in the United States. Quite a few of the facts concerning the atrocities by graduates of the School of the Americas have been, at times, published in the mainstream media. Yet, the School of the Americas continues to be funded by the U.S. Congress, despite efforts by Representative Joseph Kennedy of Massachusetts and others to halt this funding. In short, the betrayal of democracy and human rights, through supporting the political evil linked to the School of the Americas, is widespread; it includes a majority of representatives in Congress. Frequently, such blatant support of political evil allows and encourages persons similar to Sir John Hargreaves and Doctor Percival to perform political evil far from public scrutiny.

∼

The connection between the wish to efface or distort factual truth and political evil cannot be overemphasized. In *The Honorary Consul*, why does Colonel Perez have the wounded Doctor Plarr killed? Perez knows very well that Plarr is not one of the kidnappers of the honorary consul, Charlie Fortnum; he has probably guessed that Plarr is being held a hostage. Furthermore, he has been on friendly terms with Plarr and even comes to his funeral, at which he "had the air of being the most serious person present."[13] What seems to have worried Colonel Perez is that Doctor Plarr might disclose the factual truth—about the kidnappers and their goals, and also about the actions of the police force which he commands, including its brutal methods. Concealing this truth requires silencing Plarr, forever.

Persons who perform political evil know the dangers of factual truths. All his life, Greene saw this clearly. In all his novels that deal with political evil, factual truth is perceived as a grave danger by the wicked agents of the evil regime. Greene also stresses that, as in *The Human Factor*, one of the reasons for performing a specific evil act is to conceal facts. In *The Captain and the Enemy*, it is evident that Mr. Quigly arranges the accident that will kill Jim so that the facts that Jim might have learned about him as a CIA agent will disappear. The same is true of the attempts to kill Arthur Rowe in *The Ministry of Fear*. Greene repeatedly shows the appalling ease with which persons involved in politics, including in democracies, attempt to efface factual truth. When, in *The Honorary Consul*, Fortnum tells the facts of Plarr's death to Mr. Critcham, an officer serving in the British Embassy, Critcham quickly dismisses the evidence. Consequently, Greene's novels suggest that presenting the factual truths about political evil is itself a way of fighting it.

～

In summary, many of Graham Greene's novels are works of art that contain a blunt political statement, much as Pablo Picasso's painting "Guernica" is a work of art that contains a political statement. Almost all Greene's novels confront political evil straightforwardly, condemning both its instigators and its performers. They especially condemn institutions that demand that people stay in their own boxes—so as to maximize harmony—and never question the major and minor policies of the institution, even if they appear to be evil. Such writing, over half a century in which political evil was rampant, testifies to Greene's courage, political responsibility, and moral integrity.

Unfortunately, it is precisely these precious qualities, which repeatedly appear in his novels, that the works of scholarship on Greene's novels that I have scrutinized have chosen to ignore. It is this ignoring that makes these scholarly works unfaithful to the spirit of Greene's writing and, as such, banal.

Put differently, none of the scholarly works on Graham Greene that I have encountered mentions what many of Greene's readers grasp: By poignantly describing many instances of political evil, Greene's wonderful novels often can serve as a beacon that enlightens much of the sordid political landscape that we daily encounter. These works of art also point out to us, the simple people of the world, that it is important to fight political evil, every day and wherever it raises its ugly head.

NOTES

1. See, for instance, Noam Chomsky, *Necessary Illusions: Thought Control in Democratic Societies* (Boston: South End Press, 1989); Noam Chomsky, *Deterring Democracy* (London: Verso, 1991); and Noam Chomsky, *Year 501: The Conquest Continues* (Boston: South End Press, 1993).

2. Graham Greene, *Yours Etc.: Letters to the Press, 1945–1989*, intro. Christopher Hawtree (London: Penguin, 1989); Marie-Françoise Allain, *Conversations with Graham Greene* (London: Penguin, 1991); Henry J. Donaghy, ed., *Conversations with Graham Greene* (Jackson: University Press of Mississippi, 1992).

3. Richard Kelly, *Graham Greene* (New York: Fredrick Ungar, 1984), 44, 70.

4. Mario Couto, *Graham Greene: On the Frontier* (New York: St. Martin's Press, 1988), 217.

5. Ibid., 225.

6. Greene, *Yours Etc.*, 130.

7. For a brief historical description of the role of the United States in the political evil in Haiti, see Noam Chomsky, "Democracy Enhancement Part II: The Case of Haiti," *Z Magazine* 7: 7/8 (July/August 1994), 52–65.

8. Graham Greene, *The Quiet American* (Middlesex, England: Penguin, 1962), 174.

9. *The Basic Works of Aristotle* (New York: Random House, 1941), 1127.

10. See, for instance, Heinrich Böll, *The Safety Net*, trans. Leila Vennewitz (Middlesex, England: Penguin, 1983); Nadine Gordimer, *A World of Strangers* (Middlesex, England: Penguin, 1962).

11. Roy Bourgeois, "School of Assassins," *Z Magazine* 7: 9 (September 1993), 14.

12. Ibid., 14–15. For additional material on the legacy of murder, oppression, and violation of human rights by graduates of the School of the Americas, see W. E. Gutman, "Politics of Assassination," *Z Magazine* 8: 9 (September 1995), 54–59.

13. Graham Greene, *The Honorary Consul* (New York: Simon and Schuster, 1973), 300.

4
Fanaticism

In one of his essays, Martin Buber relates the fable of a man inspired by God who fled the realms of human intercourse:

> There he wandered till he came to the gates of the mystery. He knocked. From within came the cry: "What do you want here?" He said, "I have proclaimed your praise in the ears of mortals but they were deaf to me. So I come to you that you yourself may hear me and reply." "Turn back," came the cry from within. "Here is no ear for you. I have sunk my hearing in the deafness of mortals."[1]

Andre Rycker, in Greene's novel *A Burnt-Out Case*, is a person who believes that he loves God and attempts to perform His wishes daily. Nevertheless, Rycker persistently flees from genuine dialogue with anyone he encounters. He never listens to other people; he never attempts to comprehend what they are trying to convey when they speak to him; he is totally insensitive to their responses, their feelings, their thoughts, their search for a worthy life. He never speaks to other persons; instead he speaks to *the idea of these persons* that he has framed in his mind. This approach is especially evident in all of Rycker's interactions with Marie, his wife, and with the "burnt-out" architect, Querry. The possibility to respond with sensitivity, to relate dialogically, comes up. Rycker evades it.

At their first meeting, Querry indicates that he would not call himself a Catholic. Rycker ignores the statement and spreads myths and lies about the architect's ardent devotion and profound dedication to Catholicism. At that meeting, Querry also intimates that perhaps Rycker should be more sensitive to Marie's difficult situation—even if, as Rycker holds, she seems deaf to his love of God. Rycker is adamant; he rejects the possibility that he might correct his actions. Later in the novel, Rycker's resolute flight from dialogue, coupled with his fervent belief that he loves God and is performing God's wishes, helps him to justify the evil that he does to Marie and Querry. In a word, Rycker is a fanatic. He holds that his belief in God justifies his actions, which include callously destroying the freedom of other people. As Greene shows, fanatics like Rycker transform their belief in God, or in some long-term historical goal, into a means that justifies their actions, however evil these actions may be.

A *Burnt-Out Case* also reveals some of the links between hubris and the evils of fanaticism. Rycker's hubris is the sick pride of the person who believes that he knows very well what is good for humanity and for all the people he meets. But humanity and people are often deaf to the fanatic's appeals. In Greene's novels, such hubris is an attitude that will often nurture fanaticism. Rycker is not an isolated case. One need only open a newspaper to discover that fanaticism and hubris are common partners in performing evil. This pattern holds true not only in those Moslem countries, such as Iran, where the resurgence of militant Islam leads to, among other evils, the enslaving of women and a brutal, violent jihad against nonbelievers. In the United States, the recent murders of medical doctors who perform abortions by members of the anti-abortion movement is an example of criminal acts in a democracy, performed by vile fanatics whose hubris is blatant. The same is true of the recent murder of Yitzchak Rabin, prime minister of Israel, by a right-wing Jewish religious fanatic who believed that he was doing God's will. As I shall soon show, a variation of this hubris emerges in the attitude of the lieutenant in *The Power and the Glory*.

The responses of Querry, Dr. Colin, and all the priests at the leper colony, except Father Thomas, to Rycker is a partially veiled contempt. (Father Thomas is also sure that he knows the truth and never listens to others; he is on the verge of fanaticism and identifies quite easily with Rycker's words and deeds.) Callous and proud, Rycker never perceives the widespread, hardly concealed scorn of many of those he encounters toward his acts and statements. He is as impregnable as a basalt column. Impregnability, however, is a personal choice, often linked to fanaticism, a choice that Rycker must renew every day in countless encounters with others. It is a way of life that he has chosen and continues to choose in defiance of the living persons whom he meets and the truths that stare him in the face.

The case of the individualist fanatic, Rycker, indicates that the evil of fanaticism is not confined to membership in religious creeds, nor is it limited to fundamentalist movements that encourage a violent intolerance toward nonbelievers or toward persons who do not live up to a specific dogma. The evil of fanaticism can be embraced by an individual in defiance of the religious establishment to which he professes to adhere. Rycker, the Catholic owner and manager of a coconut oil factory, is a fanatic, while the Catholic priests in the neighboring leper colony firmly reject any imposing of their views on the people whom they serve and heal. These priests understand themselves as humble strugglers seeking to bring some good into a world in which suffering abounds. No such humble struggling can be discerned in the acts and sayings of Andre Rycker.

∿

Greene does not ignore the widespread fanaticism within established religions. In *Monsignor Quixote*, he shows the evil of a dogmatic fanaticism within the Catholic Church. The dogmatic faith of the bishop and Father Herrera, as well as their relentless deification of the institution that they serve, leads to their unwillingness to relate to other persons as partners in the world. Their dogmatism and fanaticism stand in stark contrast to the wonderful friendship that slowly grows between Monsignor Quixote and the communist ex-mayor of El Toboso, Zancas, whom Father Quixote fondly calls Sancho. One characteristic of this friendship is the willingness and readiness of the two men to learn from each other. They spontaneously share their encounters with the world with each other—honestly, with mutual respect, and often joyfully. They acknowledge their profound differences of belief, but, as Martin Buber pointed out, differences are necessary for the otherness of the Other to emerge, and for genuine dialogue to come into being.

Genuine dialogue is well nigh impossible with the bishop or with Father Herrera. Their attitude toward the world and to other persons expresses no willingness to learn, to share, or even to listen carefully to a person who does not share their rigid interpretation of Catholic dogma. They only know how to develop relationships of an almost diabolic solidarity, of identification—never the love of friendship. Is Greene indicating that fanatics can only establish a demonic solidarity between them, never a genuine friendship? Definitely!

The bishop is as inert as a rock. In the first pages of the book, his dogmatism is evident; one already discerns that such dogmatism can deteriorate to fanaticism. Later, the bishop has Monsignor Quixote drugged, kidnapped, and jailed in his own house, thus destroying Monsignor Quixote's freedom. Like Rycker, the bishop refuses to listen to any fact that may challenge his fixed and inane views about Catholicism, religious faith, Spain, or what is happening in the world. The poignant historical perceptions that Karl Marx and Friedrich Engels presented in *The Communist Manifesto* are dismissed with contempt. The truths about Monsignor Quixote's travels and deeds are disparaged and discarded. Such a response is dogmatic; it becomes fanatical and evil when linked to deeds that destroy Monsignor Quixote's freedom. Someone may say that the bishop is confident that he is destroying Father Quixote's freedom so as to strengthen the Catholic Church and to ensure the respect that it deserves in the world. That only supports my point. When the Bishop totally disregards the freedom of Monsignor Quixote and listens to him only to find details that may either condemn or pardon him—in short, when a religious official cares only about the religious order or institution that he or she serves and its dogma, as the bishop does—fanaticism has triumphed.

Is it not true, however, that *Monsignor Quixote* is a comedy? Perhaps. If so, it is similar to the movies of Charlie Chaplin and to Miguel de Cervantes' great work, both of which were admired by Graham Greene. The novel uses comic effects to criticize profoundly the institutions of a depraved and decadent society and its church. Specifically, the book criticizes the ossified and cowardly Catholic Church, as well as its ardent supporters in the conservative and fascist institutions of contemporary Spain. (There is also some valid criticism of the Soviet regime and its many evils.) Thus, with the help of humor, Greene repeatedly reminds the reader that many members of the Catholic Church, like the bishop, happily support the evil regime of General Franco, despite its many atrocities. He also indicates that quite a few adherents to and officials of the Catholic establishment continue to support the evil of many conservative Spanish institutions and to be supported by these institutions.

~

A major point that unites *Monsignor Quixote* and *A Burnt-Out Case* is that the fanatic's certainty in the truth of the dogma that he or she passionately embraces can only lead to a lack of spirituality. When the Holy Office in the Vatican condemned *The Power and the Glory*, which Greene considered one of his best novels, he personally experienced the spiritual poverty of the Catholic Church.[2] I have shown elsewhere that a fanatic is a coward who blocks lucidity, respect for the truth, and clear thinking.[3] The bishop and Rycker are examples of fanatics who persistently flee lucidity, truth, and clear thinking. Such a flight probably characterized those Vatican officials who decided to condemn *The Power and the Glory*. Greene shows that an intentional embracing of ignorance and superficiality in relating to concrete reality constitutes such a persistent flight; no spirituality will emerge in this wasteland of shallowness and ignorance.

The flight from lucidity, truth, and clear thinking is linked to the spiritual poverty of the interpersonal relations mentioned above. In *A Burnt-Out Case*, neither Rycker nor Parkinson cares about truth or about lucidly perceiving themselves or the world. They are incapable of the simple dialogue, the love, and the sharing that are the basis of genuine friendship. Doctor Colin and Querry do care about truth, lucidity, and clear thinking; they slowly establish a friendship, despite Querry's being a burnt-out case. In *Monsignor Quixote*, the bishop and Father Herrera cannot relate to a person who questions Catholic dogma. Such a person can only be branded a heretic. These Catholic priests do not need to strive to be lucid or to pursue truth, since they are certain that truth is and will always be in their pocket, in the interpretation of the Scriptures to which they adhere.

In contrast, both Monsignor Quixote and the communist, Sancho, are willing to question the dogmas and principles central to their existence. At times comically, but always persistently, they seek truth and lucidity. This willingness to seek truth and lucidity requires sharing a sense of doubt about their deepest beliefs, even with people who question the tenets central to their existence. This sharing of doubt helps Monsignor Quixote and the mayor, Sancho, to establish a worthy friendship. Consider this incident:

> The Mayor put his hand for a moment on Father Quixote's shoulder, and Father Quixote could feel the electricity of affection in the touch. It's odd, he thought, as he steered Rocinante with undue caution round a curve, how sharing a sense of doubt can bring men together even more than sharing a faith. The believer will fight another believer over a shade of difference: the doubter fights only with himself.[4]

Doubt, coupled with a lucid search for truth, and with authentic caring for other persons in the world, makes a place in the world for other doubters. Greene reemphasizes this point at the end of *Monsignor Quixote*. He introduces Father Leopoldo, the Trappist who has reached faith through studying and accepting René Descartes' philosophy, which is based on doubt. Unlike the bishop and Father Herrera, Father Leopoldo cares profoundly about other people. He is open to dialogue and to friendship.

In contrast, a fanatic's belief forcefully evicts all nonbelievers from the world that the fanatic shares with them. At times, as in some instances of Islamic jihad or in the Oklahoma City bombing in the United States, the fanatic dutifully murders, maims, and inflicts physical suffering upon these evicted nonbelievers. The only matter that worries the bishop after he hears that Monsignor Quixote has been injured in a car accident and is recovering in the Osera Monastery of the Trappists is that his orders be fulfilled: that Father Quixote not be allowed to say Mass, even in private. No consideration as to Father Quixote's health troubles this fervent fanatic. The bishop has already forcefully evicted Monsignor Quixote from the world that they have previously shared. Why need he be concerned with his health or his well-being?

Another reason it is difficult to establish friendship with a fanatic is that, as Greene vividly shows, the fanatic is a terrible bore. That should not arouse wonder. Rycker and the bishop are monological persons who extract from reality what they need to justify their dogmas. They refuse to acknowledge that the world includes surprises. The only thing that concerns them is holding on to their power and to the possibility of continuing to present their monologues. No meaningful discussion in which one learns or attains worthy insights can emerge in interaction with a monological person. Listening to such a person, Greene subtly suggests in *A Burnt-Out Case*, is like being forced to hear the continual croaking of jungle frogs, who from afar echo the hollow phrases that the fanatic repeatedly enunciates.[5]

∼

For a young person, embracing fanaticism can be a way of rebelling against obvious evils that he or she perceives and refuses to ignore. For centuries, the Catholic Church in Mexico and in other Central and South American countries firmly supported the powerful and the wealthy who brutally plundered, oppressed, killed, and cruelly exploited the indigenous poor.[6] Rebelling against this terrible evil of the Catholic Church, which termed itself a godly institution, leads the lieutenant in *The Power and the Glory* to adopt an anti-Catholic materialist fanaticism. Note, however, that, in contrast to the devout Catholic fanatics (Rycker, the bishop, and Father Herrera), whom Greene describes as uncaring, inane, monological persons, the lieutenant sincerely cares about his fellow Mexicans. His fanatical anti-Catholicism arises as a genuine response to the horror of the evils that he perceives and that the Catholic Church and its many priests unscrupulously support.

The lieutenant's profound hatred of Catholic priests, coupled with his willing-ness to take hostages from among the peasants and to kill them so as to capture the whiskey priest—this hatred is mingled with compassion for the suffering of the poor Mexicans with whom he grew up. Relentlessly pursuing the priest, he learns that he himself has chosen a difficult, lonely way of life. He senses vaguely that his brutality and persistence in wishing to kill the fleeing whiskey priest is leading him astray, away from the people whom he wants to assist, away from the poverty-stricken Mexicans to whom he wishes to restore their stolen property and integrity. Seeds of doubt as to the path he has chosen emerge in the lieutenant's consciousness. Aware of his freedom and responsibility, he senses that he cannot flee despair and anguish. As mentioned, no such doubts or anguish as to their chosen way of life inform the bishop, Father Herrera, or Rycker. Their fanaticism has metastasized throughout their being.

What is the lieutenant's mistake? It emerges in a discussion with the whiskey priest at the end of the novel. The lieutenant attacks the priest and the Catholic Church for supporting the rich and ignoring their brutal oppression and continual plundering of the poor. He blames the whiskey priest for deceiving the poor about the evident reasons for their suffering. The priest attempts to reason his way out of this condemnation.

> "I hate your reasons," the lieutenant said. "I don't want reasons. If you see somebody in pain, people like you reason and reason. You say—pain's a good thing, perhaps he'll be better for it one day. I want to let my heart speak."
> "At the end of a gun."
> "Yes. At the end of a gun."
> "Oh well, perhaps when you're my age you'll know the heart's an untrustworthy beast."[7]

Greene frequently shows that the heart is an untrustworthy beast. His novels reveal that wicked fanatics often say that they are following their hearts. In *The Human Factor*, an evil supporter and enforcer of apartheid, Cornelius Muller, the South African Secret Service high officer who wants to use tactical atomic weapons against the indigenous rebelling blacks in South Africa, believes that he is speaking from the heart. It is his heart that guides the otherwise prudent Muller to believe that the rules of apartheid will reign in Heaven. Innocent unrebelling blacks will be allotted "their own kind of heaven."[8] Here Greene shows how easily fanaticism and political evil blend in a so-called Western country.

Greene's novels indicate that the heart frequently expresses pity and compassion, yet it rarely shows the way to struggle against evil. Beyond the expression of feelings, the heart often misleads. To fight evil while doing as little evil as possible, a person should have a conception of the Good and an idea of how to attempt honestly to bring forth that Good in the situation in which one struggles. The conception of the Good is often vague, as with Fowler in *The Quiet American*. In *The Power and the Glory*, the lieutenant's conception of the Good is confined and abstract; it is quite detached from the situation in which he struggles and from the people with whom he shares his life. It is a negation of a negation that does not become an affirmation.

The lieutenant senses that his abstract conception of the Good is alien to the people to whom he wishes to bring that Good. He reaches out to his fellow Mexicans and is repeatedly rebuffed. More and more, he relies on what his heart speaks and on the newly made laws of the state. He refuses to entertain doubt as to the dictates of his heart or of the laws. It is this refusal that allows him to kill innocent hostages and, later, to shoot the whiskey priest after a kangaroo trial. These deeds alienate him even further from his fellow Mexicans.

In one of the last scenes in the book, a young boy spits on the lieutenant's revolver. The boy perhaps senses that the lieutenant's fervent belief in what his heart speaks, which allows the killing of innocent people, is an evil expression of pride. It is hubris. Although he does not learn from his perceptions, even the lieutenant perceives that such fervent, unquestioning belief and pride frequently bring much evil, including the personal destruction of one's sensitivity to other persons.

Put otherwise, unlike Rycker, the bishop, and Father Herrera, who merely arouse our disgust, the lieutenant is a tragic figure. He does not acknowledge that proudly following the dictates of his heart and the laws of the state can bring great ruin. He somewhat resembles Scobie, that pious Catholic police officer in *The Heart of the Matter*, whose pride and pity lead him to choose suicide instead of confronting other people with the truth. As Sophocles points out in the last verses of *Antigone*, such hubris is divorced from wisdom. Indeed, the killings and the self-destruction brought about by the lieutenant's acts are similar, although perhaps less extreme, than the harsh and evil deeds of Creon that lead to his own downfall in Sophocles' tragedy.

~

Greene's novels bear a clear message: Fanaticism is here—in our own society and in many other societies of the world. It blends with other evils and constantly wreaks havoc on the Good while destroying the soul of the fanatic. We must constantly fight these evils and educate others to reject them firmly.

How do we fight fanaticism and the evils described in previous chapters of this section? An answer emerges in the next section where I consider Greene's unsung heroes.

NOTES

1. Martin Buber, *Between Man and Man* (London: Fontana, 1961), 33.

2. Greene mentioned this fact in a few places. See, for instance, Henry J. Donaghy, ed., *Conversations with Graham Greene* (Jackson: University Press of Mississippi, 1992), 48–52.

3. Haim Gordon and Rivca Gordon, *Sartre and Evil: Guidelines for a Struggle* (Westport, CT: Greenwood Press, 1995). See the chapters on Jean Genet.

4. Graham Greene, *Monsignor Quixote* (London: Penguin, 1983), 59.

5. Graham Greene, *A Burnt-Out Case* (London: Penguin, 1963), 42.

6. For an enlightening study of the ruin inflicted upon Latin America with the support of the Catholic Church, see Eduardo Galeano, *Open Veins of Latin America: Five Centuries of the Pillage of a Continent* (New York: Monthly Review Press, 1973).

7. Graham Greene, *The Power and the Glory* (London: Penguin, 1962), 199.

8. Graham Greene, *The Human Factor* (London: Penguin, 1978), 157.

Part II

UNSUNG HEROES
WHO FIGHT EVIL

5
Seeing Evil

Graham Greene's unsung heroes—Ida in *Brighton Rock*, Brown in *The Comedians*, Thomas Fowler in *The Quiet American*, D. in *The Confidential Agent*, Dr. Czinner in *Stamboul Train*, and others—see evil for what it is. Greene's novels suggest that such seeing is quite exceptional. Why?

Decades earlier, in *Heart of Darkness*, Joseph Conrad poignantly described the acute loneliness of the wanderer and seaman, Marlow, who perceives the evil of Kurtz and of the other "pilgrims." These evildoers are brutally plundering Africa for ivory. Marlow, however, is far away from almost any semblance of Western civilization, in the heart of Africa, seemingly outside of history. The evil that Marlow sees seems remote, dreamlike. At the trading station deep in Africa, the European men he encounters

> wandered here and there with their absurd long staves in their hands, like a lot of faithless pilgrims bewitched inside a rotten fence. The word "ivory" rang in the air, was whispered, was sighed. You would think they were praying to it. A taint of imbecile rapacity blew through it all, like a whiff from some corpse.[1]

In contrast, almost all of Greene's unsung heroes encounter evil in the midst of contemporary history, in England, Vietnam, Haiti, Panama, Paraguay, Spain, Yugoslavia, and other countries. The imbecile rapacity that supports evil, which Marlow encounters in the heart of Africa, repeatedly emerges in what we call the civilized world. Greene's novels indicate that this evil arises from the political and personal decisions of individuals whom we may encounter in our daily interactions. Still, the novels show, many if not most people refuse to see this evil for what it is—the willful destruction of human freedom. Why? Answering this question will help us to comprehend the way of life adopted by Greene's unsung heroes.

∾

The decision to pursue their greed for ivory animates the lives of the "pilgrims" whom Marlow encounters and it seemingly blinds them to the evil that they are doing. The relentless greedy pursuit of wealth is one of the most common choices of existence that support a decision not to see evil. A coterie of rich people animated by greed who choose to be blind to evil is described in Greene's *Dr. Fischer of Geneva or The Bomb Party*. The story takes place in Switzerland, that supposed hub of impartial decency in the center of European civilization.

It is probably no coincidence that Greene chose Geneva for the home of the wicked Dr. Fischer and the greedy human "Toads" who revolve around him, attracted by his wealth. Geneva is the birthplace of Jean-Jacques Rousseau, who answered a resounding "No!" to the question whether the restoration of the arts and sciences had contributed to the purification of mankind. Geneva also housed the headquarters of the defunct League of Nations, which never countered the evils of Benito Mussolini, Adolf Hitler, and other wicked fascist leaders. It is an affluent city that for the past half-century has boasted a host of international agencies that seemingly strive to better the plight of many members of humankind whose freedom has been destroyed, very frequently by the blatant evils of capitalist nations and their leaders. It is also a city, Greene's novel suggests, to which today's rich and greedy gravitate, probably because an atmosphere of indifference to evils such as that of Dr. Fischer prevails there.

In this throbbing heart of European civilization, Dr. Fischer conducts his pernicious experiments on the cupidity of the rich. The experiments reveal that the stinking-rich "Toads" are an asinine elite whose unbridled greed leads them to refuse persistently to see Dr. Fischer's evil. They grovel before Dr. Fischer and willingly give up all integrity as long as he awards them expensive presents that partially satisfy their greed. Is the existential choice of the "Toads"—persistently refusing to see evil so as to justify their greed—exceptional in contemporary Swiss and European society? As an example I will soon cite reveals, not at all!

Let me now suggest what should be evident. To see evil and to fight it courageously, one must forcefully reject greed! All of Greene's unsung heroes are not greedy persons, nor are they very wealthy. Dr. Fischer says clearly "All my friends are rich and the rich are the greediest. The rich have no pride except in their possessions."[2] Greed, together with pride solely in possessions, is the choice of a way of life that refuses to see the evils that one meets. Put differently, Dr. Fischer's pernicious experiments reveal that greed easily corrodes a person's integrity. As a corollary, note that, in this novel and in many others, Greene shows that people who willingly compromise their integrity will refuse to see greed and other evils—or to fight them.

∾

Dr. Fischer of Geneva or The Bomb Party may be black farce, as some critics have suggested. This farce, however, points to an all too common reality. Here is an example, from Switzerland, in which live, socially respected persons persistently refused to see evil in order to justify their greed.

In 1973, the Swiss-based pharmaceutical company, Roche, was found by the British Monopolies Commission to be "charging its British subsidiary exorbitant rates for the raw ingredients of the drugs."[3] Among other conclusions, the commission demanded that Roche pay back 12 million pounds sterling in compensation. Roche finally settled out of court and paid back 3.75 million pounds sterling. While these negotiations were taking place,

> the European Commission (EC) was building a case against Roche. . . . Large amounts of information . . . were supplied by a Roche employee, Stanley Adams, who pointed out that Roche and other major vitamin manufacturers had formed "an illegal price cartel to fix prices, agree to levels of production and share the vitamin market between themselves." The EC decided to focus on Roche's further activity in setting up "fidelity contracts." . . . In 1976 Roche was found guilty of unfair trading practices and given a small fine.
>
> Adams was subsequently arrested by the Swiss Authorities, at Roche's instigation, and three weeks after the company was found guilty Adams too was convicted on charges of persistent economic espionage and persistently betraying trade secrets. As a result of his arrest, his wife, who had been told that he faced up to 20 years in prison, committed suicide.[4]

The story of Stanley Adams and Roche could easily have served as the model for *Dr. Fischer of Geneva or The Bomb Party*. Many members of Swiss society refused to see the evil of Roche, probably because of their own personal greed, despite the fact that the illegality of Roche's greed and its criminal behavior toward millions of consumers was evident and despite the fact that the company was found guilty by the EC. The conviction of Stanley Adams is a striking example of the refusal to see Roche's evil by an entire society, including Swiss judges, prosecutors, journalists, and elected members of the Swiss Assembly. What is interesting in the case of Roche is that, as in Greene's novel and *Heart of Darkness*, the greed and evil of the evildoers is unconcealed. It occurred in the public space. One need only decide to see it in order to condemn it.

∼

The linkage between greed and the choice not to see evil suggests a principle that emerges repeatedly in Greene's novels. Seeing evil is linked to a person's daily choices and way of life, to his or her being-in-the-world. As a simple example, consider the difference between Alfred Jones and the Toads in *Dr. Fischer of Geneva or The Bomb Party*. The Toads prize only their possessions and are daily concerned with attaining more material goods; as a result of this decision, they forfeit their personal integrity and refuse to see evil. Alfred Jones has chosen an existence in which he cherishes truth and love. An immediate result is that Jones is able to express genuine love, and he despises any vile manipulation of human beings, such as what always occurs at Dr. Fischer's famous parties.

Consequently, Alfred Jones can virtually spit upon Dr. Fischer's evil acts and defy his mad antics. He wants no part of Dr. Fischer's wealth. He is not an unsung hero, for, in the novel, he does not fight evil straightforwardly. Nevertheless, he sees evil for what it is. He daily makes the simple and difficult choices that, under certain circumstances, might bring him to act heroically.

More complex is a comparison between Alden Pyle and Thomas Fowler in *The Quiet American*. Pyle is not greedy, so why does he not see the evil that he is doing? How is his being-in-the-world linked to the evil that he does? Consider Pyle's initiating the bombing of the center of Saigon, in which dozens of innocent Vietnamese people are mutilated and killed. The bombing is a result of Pyle's decision to set up a Third Force in Vietnam, to arm it, to encourage it to obtain power, and to sanction its violent and evil deeds. If successful, Pyle believes, the Third Force will help the United States to dominate and exploit all of Indochina. Surrounded by the corpses and mutilated bodies of the victims of the bomb, Fowler tries to point out to Pyle the horror that has resulted from his bizarre deeds. He angrily accuses him. Pyle sees nothing. In his own mind, he remains innocent. Confronted with Pyle's desensitized being, Fowler concludes: "What's the good? he'll always be innocent, you can't blame the innocent, they are always guiltless. All you can do is control them or eliminate them. Innocence is a kind of insanity."[5]

Greene is right. In the twentieth century, large groups of sophisticated intellectuals, government officers and agents, and many other persons have chosen to live an insane version of innocence, which they firmly believe allows them to be guiltless—whatever evil they do. These insane innocents have decided to be blind to evil. Even when a person does evil, even when the horror of one's deeds is strewn before one's eyes, like the bleeding, mutilated bodies of innocent Vietnamese that lie wounded and dead around Pyle, these inculpable innocent evildoers see nothing. One of the finest existential choices of all of Greene's unsung heroes is their refusal to condone or support this insane innocence. Often, like Fowler, they fight to open the eyes of others to the evil that they have instigated. They attempt to stop this evil. They often fail.

Why is Pyle's innocence insane? Note that Pyle refuses to establish relations of genuine reciprocity with other human beings. Sympathy, empathy, and sharing his being with nonwhites is not a possibility that he even considers. (Phuong seems to be an exception, but Pyle also merely manipulates her.) Genuine dialogue and the sharing of doubts are totally alien to his being-in-the-world. Pyle relates to all persons whom he encounters merely as means for his own ends. That is the essence of what Greene calls Pyle's insanity.

Make no mistake, however. Such insanity is a choice, not a neurosis or a predicament. A person who chooses an existence in which all other human beings are merely means to an end is often called selfish or egocentric. Greene goes further. He suggests that, in cases similar to that of Alden Pyle, this choice is a determined refusal to share the world genuinely with other human beings. It is a stubborn decision to live in a world constructed by one's fantasies, irrational thinking, and abstract ideas. The gains of such a choice are significant. Since he is always faithful to the products of his mind, Pyle will never see the evil that his decisions bring. Consequently, whatever evil Pyle does, as long as he remains faithful to the world of his fantasies, he seemingly remains innocent!

Some may suggest that Pyle can act with nobility; after all, he courageously saves the wounded Fowler. His is a false nobility. It has been endlessly repeated that courage in war does not ensure a noble existence. Valor in war often has nothing to do with civil and personal courage, which emerges when a person seeks to live a worthy life, including, for instance, the pursuit of justice or wisdom. Such a worthy life demands reciprocity, which is alien to Pyle's being-in-the-world. According to this being-in-the-world, Pyle must present a facade of bravery and fair play toward other white people. This facade prompts his brave acts under enemy fire. Despite his fair play and bravery, however, Pyle persistently chooses an existence in which he relates to all people as means to his own ends.

~

Alden Pyle's choice of a mad innocence supports his belief that the worst thing he can do is to bungle the way he uses other persons. Note that Pinkie in *Brighton Rock* also grasps the failure of some of his evil deeds as mere bungling. Pyle is an educated and sophisticated CIA agent, not a petty criminal, but in his mad innocence, he resembles Pinkie.

Here is a major point that concerns the evil instigated by many institutions and companies, such as Roche, including numerous institutions in democratic regimes. Pyle has been taught that, if he remains faithful to the CIA, the worst that he may be accused of is poor judgment or clumsiness. Since he firmly believes that the CIA serves the good of all mankind, then by definition, he is never guilty. The sensitive reader, however, perceives that Pyle's supposed innocence merely conceals his culpability of always relating to other people as means and of deliberately ignoring their freedom and integrity. Such a faith in the blessings brought to humankind by the CIA, coupled with the concealing of his personal guilt, allows Pyle to choose unconcernedly to destroy the lives and freedom of innocent Vietnamese.

Pyle's insane innocence is so widespread that it requires further elaboration. Consider an imaginary situation. How would we respond if Alden Pyle walked into the center of Saigon and shot and hand-grenaded three dozen Vietnamese passersby because he had supposedly heard the voice of Jesus or Muhammed encouraging him to go on a killing rampage? When captured, Pyle would testify that he went on his murderous spree because of his faith in Jesus' or Muhammed's message. We would conclude that Pyle was insane and hence guiltless.

Alden Pyle hears no religious luminary. Instead he reads York Harding on the Third Force and finds him intellectually stimulating; he has deep faith in York Harding's thesis, which he sees as being beyond criticism. That faith is fanatical. In Pyle's eyes, the truth of York Harding's thesis renders him guiltless, no matter what he does to the Vietnamese people, including bombing innocent men and women in the center of Saigon. Let me emphasize this point. Thanks to York Harding, whose work shows him that history is definitely on his side, Pyle refuses to see evil; as long as he follows York Harding's tenets, he perceives himself as forever innocent. Such a perceived innocence regardless of one's evil deeds, which is probably embraced by most government agents, is indeed a kind of insanity. Let me reiterate, however. This semblance of insanity is not a sickness. It is an existential decision to relate to all other people merely as means that serve one's own theories or fantasies of a world order. In a word, Pyle is responsible and hence guilty.

Like many a psychotic, Pyle refuses to listen to the voices of living persons whom he encounters or to comprehend the horrors of a conspicuous evil that he has instigated. Unlike many psychotics, however, Pyle knows very well what he is doing. Listening to Thomas Fowler and seeing these horrors could lead Pyle to doubt some of his assumptions about the historical reality in which he fervently believes. Perhaps it might lead him to doubt a basic tenet of his existence—that all other people exist merely to serve as means to his ends. No such doubt emerges in Pyle's mind, despite Fowler's many attempts to educate him.

A major reason that Fowler is an unsung hero is that he sees Pyle's evil for what it is and decides to halt him, even if it means having him murdered.

～

As Greene shows through the decisions of Thomas Fowler, Dr. Czinner in *Stamboul Train*, and other unsung heroes, seeing evil is often linked to a groping and, at times, blundering attempt to stop that evil while struggling to live lucidly and authentically. By their actions, Greene's unsung heroes indicate, however, that there is no vicious circle here. Rather, one of the lessons that Fowler learns while struggling against Pyle is that seeing specific evils when one encounters them and living authentically and lucidly are two sides of the same coin. To live authentically and lucidly, one must be willing to see a specific evil face to face; seeing that specific evil requires living lucidly and authentically.

Consider Ida in *Brighton Rock*. She slowly picks her way toward discovering the guilt of Pinkie. She embarks upon this groping path after she perceives the mysterious death of Charles Hale for what it is—a murder. She had liked Charles Hale—"Fred," as she called him. She is angered by his being murdered, and she wants those who performed this act brought to justice. Note that Ida is radically different from Alden Pyle, in that she does not view other persons as means to her own ends but rather as partners who share the world with her. Her response to the evil done to Hale is authentic, with no trace of bad faith, even if pursuing the murderer includes consulting a Ouija Board and betting on Black Boy in a horse race.

Through her persistent reconnoitering and poking around, Ida learns vaguely of Pinkie's involvement in Hale's murder. She also sees Pinkie's other evil actions, especially his deceitful manipulating of Rose. Seeing Pinkie's wicked deeds encourages Ida to continue her struggle to halt his evil acts. She hopes to save Rose from the evil that she foresees and, perhaps, to bring Pinkie to justice. Guided by her simple knowledge of right from wrong, Ida refuses to let those responsible for crimes and evil flee from their guilt and condemnation. She is lucid, authentic, and sees evil.

Unfortunately, Ida's seeing evil, her simply knowing right from wrong, her prying into the lives of others so as to stop wicked deeds, and, yes, her persistent struggle against Pinkie's blatant wickedness have angered quite a few celebrated academics who have discussed Greene's novels. Together with discrediting and berating Ida, these respected scholars reject the significance of seeing evil and the need to struggle against it. As Graham Greene repeatedly shows, however, in relation to evil, there is no middle way. Either you fight it or you support it. Hence, the illustrious academics who condemn Ida are, in a word, supporters of evil. To justify their support, some of these scholars even adulate what they call Pinkie's "pure" evil.

As I have repeatedly stated, such scholarly support of evil enrages me. Evil is evil, and, in my humble view, deserves to be negated, eradicated, and fought wherever it raises its ugly head. No amount of scholarship should desensitize people to evils that stare them in the face, like the brutal, violent attacks upon innocent Nicaraguans by the contras, supported by the United States and especially by Ronald Reagan—an evil that Graham Greene forcefully condemned. Furthermore, an interpretation of Greene's novels that does not straightforwardly reject all evil is grotesquely false and inane. Hence, to support the truths that Greene vividly presents, it is important to digress briefly and to reject one such example of desensitized, seemingly innocent, scholarly writing about Pinkie and Ida.

Terry Eagleton has written, "Pinkie regards human involvement as despicable weakness, and is damned for it; yet the novel's major image of such involvement is the despicable Ida."[6] Make no mistake. Eagleton agrees with Pinkie that Ida is despicable. He never pays tribute to her relentless attempts to save Rose from Pinkie's wicked manipulations or her struggle to discover who murdered Charles Hale. Simple people, like Ida, who care enough about right and wrong to attempt to do something about an evil staring them in the face, do not fit into Eagleton's sophisticated literary models. Indeed, like other writers about Greene's novels mentioned in previous chapters, seeing evil or fighting specific evils does not concern Eagleton.

To justify his admiration of Pinkie and his viewing Ida as despicable, Eagleton has developed a pseudo-metaphysical approach that endows Pinkie's murderous acts and performing of evil with integrity and innocence. Consider two additional sentences from the paragraph by Eagleton that ends with the above citation:

> Pinkie may be "evil," but he is not "corrupt"; his evil is a pure pristine integrity, a priestly asceticism which refuses the contaminations of ordinary living. . . . Pinkie *is* innocent, but while he is damned for it, it is also a mark of his superiority to the Ida Arnolds of the world.[7]

Let the reader insert in these sentences, instead of Pinkie, names like Adolf Hitler, Joseph Stalin, Ronald Reagan, and other political leaders whose wicked decisions have brought death and suffering to millions of innocent human beings. That is an easy exercise that shows the poverty of Eagleton's pseudo-metaphysics.

A bit more difficult is asking this question: What distorted mind will attempt to justify the idea that a murderer of innocent people can be endowed with "evil [that] is a pure pristine integrity"? Where else is it stated that a murderer "*is* innocent" and superior "to the Ida Arnolds of the world"? There is one prominent answer in the twentieth century. Such an adulation and admiration of "pure" evil, such a bizarre rejection of simple people who struggle for what is right, was repeatedly expressed in Nazi ideology. During the Nazi era, Hitler's Nazi pundits repeatedly explained that the *Führer's* evil was pure, had integrity, and was metaphysically superior to the "foolish do-gooders" who condemned Hitler's deeds.

It is evident that this new scholarly version of Nazism is a gross misinterpretation of Graham Greene's novels. It is a vile creation, born of Eagleton's snobbish, desensitized thinking. It was sanctioned by the editor of the volume in which the essay appears, Harold Bloom. Both are responsible for this wicked, malformed, seemingly innocent scholarship. Let me state clearly. Graham Greene, who throughout his life and in all his writings emphatically rejected and fought evil, deserves a less evil and stupid reading of his novels than that provided by these celebrated scholars.

We can now return to Ida Arnold and *Brighton Rock*. She is a vivacious reminder that seeing evil has little to do with academic scholarship. Unfortunately, as the insidious and pernicious work of Eagleton and Bloom reveals, we are often in dire need of such reminders. As already mentioned, I have recently discussed elsewhere, in some detail, the inauthenticity of academics and their cowardly responses in relating to evil that stares them in the face. Nonetheless, I think it important to add a personal note here as well.[8]

I am tenured at Ben Gurion University in Beer Sheva, Israel. Together with other Israelis, I have been working for years for the human rights of the Palestinians in the Gaza Strip. Not one of the other ten Israelis with whom I have been fortunate to struggle against the evident evils of Israeli oppression in the Gaza Strip is a faculty member of Ben Gurion University. Note that Ben Gurion University has 600 professors and is situated thirty-five miles from the Gaza Strip. Moreover, in the process of fighting the evils done by Israelis in the Gaza Strip (and also other evils), I have met many admirable people like Ida, who intuitively know right from wrong and are willing to fight for what is right. Describing such people as despicable, as Eagleton does, is vile. It is also the epitome of academic hubris.

In terms of Graham Greene's novels, the approach expressed in Eagleton's writing very much resembles the evil approach to life adopted by Alden Pyle. Both Eagleton and Pyle embrace a superficial academic model that helps them *not* to see evil and to flee from responsibility for the world that we share with others. As Greene shows, this may be a first step in embracing an innocent madness that supports evil.

~

Brown, the hotelier in *The Comedians*, is willing to deceive others throughout his lonely and transient life. This deceiving, however, does not interfere with Brown's seeing evil or with his appreciating the Good, as his warm relations with Doctor Magiot reveal. The final letter from Doctor Magiot says clearly that Brown has had the courage never to be indifferent; in that, he resembles his mother. Brown is not indifferent because he strives, as best he can, not to deceive himself. A person who daily struggles against self-deception, as philosophers from Socrates to Sartre have pointed out, cannot be indifferent to evil. Put otherwise, to live in indifference to the widespread brutal evils that prevail in our world, individuals must lie to themselves and diligently embrace bad faith.

Greene vividly shows that the struggle for truth in relation to oneself requires courage; the flight into indifference and bad faith is an act of cowardice. To camouflage their cowardice, bad faith, and indifference, many people comprehend life as a stage upon which they, together with other comedians, strut and stagger, acting out parts. Like Jones in *The Comedians*, or Alden Pyle, or Aunt Augusta, some of these comedians are so engrossed with playing their parts that self-deception becomes a way of life, a commitment, in addition to being a manner of seducing others. Bad faith has totally infected these characters' being-in-the-world. Still, Greene indicates that it is possible to transcend the role of being a comedian. How? The life of Doctor Magiot provides an answer: by living in good faith, by caring for others, and by assuming responsibility for what may be called 'the fate of the world' in that small area upon the earth where one finds oneself.

A person like Brown, who courageously struggles to live in good faith and who rejects indifference, will not sink into cynicism, nor will he or she become a sycophant. Make no mistake, however. Brown has many hang-ups. In his relations with Martha Pineda, he is mistrustful, envious, ironic, and often stupid. He misses the opportunity for true love and genuine joyful sharing that she offers him, even if for a short time. Martha's trust, love, and wisdom impress him only in retrospect. Despite his nagging myopia, despite his ruinous envy, his jaundice, and his foolish suspicions, Martha loves Brown. She perceives that he is genuine—never indifferent, either to her or to the world. By being genuine, he attains an integrity that her husband and many other men never obtain.

Brown's authentic life and integrity are natural outcomes of his struggle for lucidity, especially in relation to himself, and of his forcefully negating all manner of self-deceit, even in the most difficult moments of his life. His integrity shines in the darkness of Haiti through his persistent refusal to be blind to the horrors of political evil that stare him in the face. He always strives to stare down the evildoers in the Tontons Macoute, who hide their wicked visages behind dark sunglasses. Despite the prevalence of evil and corruption in Haiti, he never becomes accustomed to its horrors; he relentlessly perceives the atrocities instigated by Papa Doc Duvalier and his brutal Tontons Macoute. In short, central to Brown's lucidity and integrity is his decision to see evil, and his seeing evil sustains his integrity, lucidity, and courage.

Martha Pineda's love for Brown is illuminating. As Greene shows in the characters of Petit Pierre and Martha's husband, persons who exist in perpetual indifference and self-deception turn themselves into spiritual dwarfs. Such inauthentic pygmies can interact with each other only as comedians *manqués* in the arena of life. Unlike Charlie Chaplin and other genuine comedians, they never challenge evil. Martha seeks true love; she can relate only to a person with integrity. She soon learns that Brown's life is desultory, yet, thanks to his striving to live in good faith and his caring about the world, he has not lost the spark of humanity that glows when a person courageously challenges evil, to use a phrase from Martin Buber. This glowing spark, which Brown himself often casually dismisses, endears him to Martha, the Smiths, Doctor Magiot, and others.

Is Greene indicating that a necessary but not sufficient condition for true love and genuine sharing is that both participants in a loving relationship see evil and courageously challenge it? Indeed he is. Look again at *Dr. Fischer of Geneva or The Bomb Party*, in which the true love and genuine joyful sharing of Anna-Luise Fischer and Alfred Jones is contrasted with the blighted love of her mother, Anna Fischer, and Mr. Steiner. Neither Anna Fischer nor Mr. Steiner has the courage to challenge the cynical brutality and fiendish evil of Dr. Fischer. Without the resoluteness to defy and resist Dr. Fischer's cruelty and iniquity, their loving relationship and lives wilt, like a tender flower in a scorching khamsin. Mr. Steiner's decision to accost Dr. Fischer and to spit in his face many years after his wicked deeds is too little, too late.

Anna-Luise has learned a major truth from her mother's sad demise: You must never evade seeing evil and you must profoundly hate evil persons, like the ruthless Dr. Fischer, every minute of your life. Never endeavor to understand these diabolical representatives of Satan, because your supposed understanding can begin to block your ability to see evil and—no less important—to spontaneously express love. Anna-Luise's hatred of her evil father has the cleanliness and innocence of childish trust in the world. This seemingly childish trust in the world is also central to true love and to a genuine sharing of the world with others. Such an engulfing trust manifests itself in the lives of those characters in Greene's novels who express love and authentic sharing: Martha Pineda, Doctor Magiot, Monsignor Quixote, Sancho, Rose Cullen in *The Confidential Agent*, and many others.

Someone may say: You started this chapter by pointing out that seeing evil is quite exceptional. You argued that seeing evil is linked to detesting evil persons, to rejecting greed, to condemning a desensitized mad innocence, to living a life of integrity, to spontaneous love, to seeking truth, to childish trust in the world, to forcefully rejecting indifference, to authenticity, and to struggling against bad faith. Are these ways of life so rare in the world?

Yes, they are! A major reason that these ways of life are exceedingly rare is the lack of courage—pure, simple courage. Graham Greene's unsung heroes are courageous. To elucidate this courage requires a new beginning.

NOTES

1. Joseph Conrad, *Heart of Darkness & The Secret Sharer* (New York: Signet, 1980), 89.

2. Graham Greene, *Dr. Fischer of Geneva or The Bomb Party* (London: Penguin, 1980), 43.

3. Andrew Chetley, *A Healthy Business? World Health and the Pharmaceutical Industry* (London: Zed Books, 1990), 24.

4. Ibid., 25.

5. Graham Greene, *The Quiet American* (Middlesex, England: Penguin, 1962), 163.

6. Terry Eagleton, "Reluctant Heroes: The Novels of Graham Greene," in Harold Bloom, ed., *Modern Critical Views: Graham Greene* (New York: Chelsea House, 1987), 117.

7. Ibid., 117.

8. Haim Gordon, *Quicksand: Israel, the Intifada, and the Rise of Political Evil in Democracies* (East Lansing: Michigan State University Press, 1995).

6
Simple Courage
and Trust in the World

W hy is Rose Cullen attracted to D. in Graham Greene's *The Confidential Agent?* When D. encounters her unreserved support for him, he asks her why she wants to help him. Rose replies " 'But it was your face. Oh,' she exclaimed, 'you ought to know how it is—there's no trust anywhere. I'd never seen a face that looked medium honest. I mean about everything.' "[1]

D. has the courage to trust the world. It is this trust, and probably his quiet courage, that Rose sees expressed upon his bleeding face after he is beaten by a brutal henchman employed by his country's enemies. She grasps that a person who trusts others is honest and can be trusted. D.'s honesty and integrity, which his face reveals, surprises and immediately attracts Rose. It resounds in the depths of her being, because it is so rare and, yes, because it is beautiful. Regardless of the amount of liquor that she has stomached, Rose sees lucidly. She grasps that trust is possible and that a person who trusts is a worthy partner in dialogue and in life. These possibilities are written on D.'s bruised face. Despite D.'s being miserably beaten up, his trust in the world is evident. It cannot be battered away.

Make no mistake, however. As a confidential agent on a dangerous mission for his besieged country, D. knows very well that he must be wary of every person he encounters. Many people will try, by crafty schemes, violent attacks, simple bribery, and other insidious and evil means, to abort his mission. They do not want D. to succeed in procuring coal for his suffering country and its legitimate government. D. strives to be scrupulous, alert, vigilant, attentive, on guard; he is often shrewd and clever. These attitudes, however, never coagulate into the slimy, deceitful inclinations and the spiritual vacuousness that constitute a mistrustful personality.

D. is often very frightened. His is a very dangerous mission. Unidentified enemies shoot at him. What is more, D. has not overcome the shell shock that he experienced when his house was bombed in the course of the civil war in his country. Still, D. trusts the world. Greene shows that this trust is a source of D.'s strength. In a world where honesty, authenticity, genuine dialogue, true love, and simple trust are very scarce, D.'s courageous honesty and trust in the world arouse respect and love in both Else and Rose Cullen. These women help him because he is honest, authentic, and trustful; as such, he is worthy of being helped. Their assistance, meager as it may seem, substantially supports D. in his difficult ongoing struggles.

As the novel progresses, D. begins to act craftily, cunningly. He lies, deceives, and misleads, but he is never steeped in mendacity. His deceptions never infect his honest way of life; instead, he chooses to lie as a necessary means in a struggle for freedom against evil, greedy, powerful foes. In that struggle, he constantly strives to retain his lucidity and authenticity. He never gives up on dialogue. When D. does develop mistrust toward someone, it is on the basis of clear evidence of that person's enmity or evil deeds. This mistrust is focused, directed toward that individual alone; it does not spill over and engulf other persons whom D. encounters.

Because it points to a specific person, D's is a lucid, even an innocent, mistrust. His deceit is what Nietzsche called an honest lie. Neither his mistrust nor his deceit clouds his perceptions of what is happening in the reality that he encounters or diminishes his seeing evil, nor does it influence his judgment. Greene shows that such deceit and mistrust are in sharp contrast to the mistrustful disposition of evil people, like the hotel manageress, who seems to live quite comfortably with her evil deeds.

I can now risk a generalization. Greene's novels repeatedly indicate that you need the courage to trust the world when you fight evil. Conversely, trust in the world is one of the crucial modes of existence in which the simple courage needed to fight evil emerges. Put succinctly, D., Rose Cullen, Doctor Magiot, Ida Arnold, Brown, Doctor Czinner, Thomas Fowler, and all of Greene's other unsung heroes are courageous people who trust the world.

~

I have not yet indicated what I mean by trust in the world. Trust in the world is basically an anti-Hobbesian attitude. It is a firm rejection of the premise that the goal of human beings living together in a commonwealth is "getting themselves out from that miserable condition of Warre, which is necessarily consequent (as hath been shewn) to the natural Passions of men."[2] Let me say it clearly. A person who trusts the world, like D., Doctor Magiot, or Ida Arnold, believes that people's natural passions or inclinations do not necessarily lead to the "miserable condition of Warre." They believe the contrary—that human passions can lead to the joy of sharing, to love, genuine community, the pursuit of justice, candid dialogue, authentic friendship, and other worthy and enhancing expressions of human existence.

Here is my definition. Trust in the world is a way of life based on the decision to regard fellow human beings as partners with whom I share this world and to whom I can entrust my being. It is a courageous and unconditional trust; no strings attached.

Note that trust in the world has nothing to do with the rigid loyalty often found among criminals who have joint interests. Criminals, as well as dedicated capitalists, accept the Hobbesian premise, and their rigid loyalty to each other is a contractual loyalty. Greene's novels frequently show the poverty of such loyalty, with its inherent mistrust, and, yes, its cowardice. Pinkie and his gang in *Brighton Rock* offer a vivid example of such loyalty and its underlying mistrust of the world. In contrast to the ruinous, untrustful way of life of Pinkie and his gang, whose criminal activities destroy the freedom of other people, in other novels Greene shows that trust in the world emerges among persons, such as D. and Rose Cullen, who struggle together to make the world a better place for all human beings.

Courageously trusting the world very often helps a person to live fully, authentically, creatively. When, at the end of *The Confidential Agent*, Rose Cullen joins D. on the small Dutch vessel in the English Channel that will carry him back to the horrors of civil war in his homeland, she is following both her love and her wish to share her life with someone whose face and existence are "medium honest." From the few words that she says at the end of the book, it is evident that Rose's love is genuine, authentic, and mature. Through her courageous decision, she unconditionally entrusts her being to D., to a mutual sharing of her life with him—until death will part them.

∼

Hold it! someone may say. Trust in the world does not ensure the finding of a worthy partner or partners with whom to share one's life. Dr. Eduardo Plarr, in Greene's *The Honorary Consul*, quite innocently trusts the world and finds no such partners. Furthermore, Plarr's life and death reveal the dangers of trusting others. Plarr unconditionally trusts his childhood friends, the kidnappers, Leon and Aquino, as persons with whom he shares the world and whose struggle for justice he supports. Later, when he acts courageously and goes out of the surrounded hut in the barrio to ask Colonel Perez to extend the hour of his ultimatum to the kidnappers, Plarr trusts Perez' fairness. Plarr's trust leads to his being shot and to his untimely death. In this novel, a poignant question emerges: Why trust the world?

It is true that trusting the world does not ensure finding a worthy partner with whom to share one's life. But living a life of mistrust blocks any possibility of finding such a partner. Of course, this is only a partial answer to the question: Why trust the world?

Before I offer a better answer, consider Plarr's mistakes. Trusting the world is not an abstract or passive way of life; it must emerge in concrete relations with specific persons encountered in one's daily engagements. It requires acting in the world, here and now. As the actions of D. and Rose in *The Confidential Agent* clearly indicate, trust in the world often arises when a person is actively involved in trying to change the world for the better. Put differently, trust in the world is frequently linked to a decision to be involved in history by fighting for the Good, while trusting other people.

Hence, Plarr's trust is, at best, problematic. His being-in-the-world is infected with a skepticism that has become ingrained. Greene indicates that this skepticism is probably rooted in what Sartre would have called Plarr's decision, during his early childhood, upon an initial project, or way of life, in which skepticism prevails.

Note that Plarr has also chosen not to involve himself wholeheartedly in the lives of the persons whom he meets. As the novel opens, he has for years been living as a detached and somewhat concerned observer. He passively comprehends what is happening, without ever engaging his whole being. It is therefore not surprising that Plarr's deep skepticism, along with the passivity that both engenders it and stems from it, blocks the possibility of his experiencing genuine love.

It should be conceded that the brutal machismo prevailing, to much applause, in Argentina and Paraguay, the many family betrayals that Plarr has witnessed, and the withered love that he has observed between his parents have probably led to his skepticism concerning the possibility of experiencing love. But Plarr makes no attempts to abandon his confining experiences or to give himself to new engagements. Throughout his life, he nurtures his skepticism, embraces it, plays with it. The reader senses that he feels quite comfortable with his skepticism, since, at least until the kidnapping, it has released him from many personal commitments. In short, skepticism constitutes Plarr's justification for his continual flight from emotional or political involvement. Indeed, Plarr never chooses involvement; at best, he agrees to be thrust into it.

Through the life of Dr. Plarr, Greene shows that skepticism is very often a lonely and ruinous path. It often creates a vicious circle. Plarr does not find true friends in Paraná, the small port city in North Argentina where he resides and practices medicine. Without true friends to whom he can entrust his being, Plarr becomes even more skeptical, and this skepticism often strangles a new possible friendship even before it can be born. It definitely ruins the loving or friendly relationship that Plarr might develop with Clara, who loves him dearly and tells him so.

Furthermore, before his encounter with the kidnappers of the honorary consul, before Leon and Aquino appear in his office, Plarr lives a passive existence. He makes no attempt to confront or even to condemn the many instances of evil that he daily encounters or that exists in Paraguay, just over the border. Thus, if Plarr trusts the world, his is an abstract, detached, half-hearted trust, with almost no concrete manifestations in his daily life. The consequences do not tarry. Unlike Rose Cullen, the world does not open new enhancing possibilities of genuine human interaction for Dr. Plarr.

~

Why trust the world? A direct answer in many of Greene's novels is that, very often, people who trust the world are able to laugh heartily, joyfully; they delight in making other people laugh with them. Joyous laughter is a manner of sharing, of spontaneously trusting other people with one's joy. Dr. Plarr is not a spontaneous person who laughs with others and expresses joy. Neither is Henry Scobie in *The Heart of the Matter*. If Scobie could laugh joyfully and spontaneously with others, if he could let go of his constant prudence, of his policing of his consciousness, perhaps he might have trusted other people with his difficulties and not fled his anguish and marital difficulties into suicide. Another example is the architect Querry in *A Burnt-Out Case*. Only when Querry begins even partially to trust the world again, after beginning to transcend his deep ennui and despair, does he begin to express himself in ways that resemble laughter. Is Greene suggesting that joyous laughter is a simple manner of expressing trust? Yes!

Yet, what about Jones in *The Comedians*, who knows how to make people laugh? Does this petty criminal and vaunting braggart trust the world? Greene shows that Jones often does trust the world. When Jones flees Captain Concasseur and the Tontons Macoute, he entrusts his being to Brown. Later he decides to join Philipot and his small untrained group of rebels, trusting them with his life. He courageously covers their retreat after they are ambushed and is killed in the process. Recalling Jones' heroism, Philipot remarks, "The men loved him. He made them laugh."[3]

Underlying the possibility of laughter is a much more decisive answer to the above question. Greene's unsung heroes indicate, through their simple courageous decisions, that we should trust the world, because that is the only way to live in freedom. Here is a direct answer from Greene's discussion of Arthur Rowe's decision to trust the brother and sister Hilfe in *The Ministry of Fear*:

> But it is impossible to go through life without trust: that is to be imprisoned in the worst cell of all, oneself. For more than a year now Rowe had been so imprisoned—there had been no change of cell, no exercise-yard, no unfamiliar warder to break the monotony of solitary confinement. A moment comes to a man when a prison-break must be made whatever the risk. Now cautiously he tried for freedom.[4]

Like Arthur Rowe, many of Greene's unsung heroes discover their freedom while struggling against evil. They learn that trust in the world is necessary to fight evil while attempting to live a worthy existence. Doctor Magiot in *The Comedians* is probably the best example of a person who trusts the world, fights evil, and tries to live a worthy life. He actively pursues justice and encourages other people to involve themselves in such pursuits as well. If asked, "Why trust the world?" Doctor Magiot would probably go beyond the quest for freedom that Arthur Rowe experiences and reply candidly, "Without trust in the world, life is not worthy of living. It becomes confined, insipid, banal, bizarre. All spirituality, all wisdom, all love vanishes!" Such a reply is partially expressed in Doctor Magiot's last letter to Brown, in which he encourages Brown not to give up faith in the possibility of changing the world for the better. Need I add that genuine faith, such as that lived and encouraged by Doctor Magiot, requires the courage to trust the world?[5]

∽

The trust in the world of Graham Greene's unsung heroes accords with a sober truth enunciated by the French writer, Paul Nizan: "False courage awaits great occasions; true courage consists of overcoming small enemies every day."[6]

Like many fanatics, Rycker in *A Burnt-Out Case* is imbued with a false courage. He awaits and even attempts to create great occasions in order, supposedly, to prove his mettle. These great occasions help Rycker to justify his distorted existence and contorted faith. Much the same can be said of the opportunistic journalist, Parkinson, who purposely adds lies to the text of the articles that he publishes in order to describe great occasions. Greene shows clearly that Rycker and Parkinson, each in his own way, do not trust the world. Another example of those who await great occasions are the greedy Toads who participate in Dr. Fischer's bomb party in *Dr. Fischer of Geneva or The Bomb Party*. They act with false courage when they pull the string that they believe will either blow them up or present them with a check for 2 million Swiss francs. But we do not need Greene's novels to witness false courage. One can perceive false courage daily merely by watching politicians, most of whom "await great occasions" to act or to issue statements.

Ida Arnold in *Brighton Rock* awaits no great occasions. She perceives that Hale's death is weird, suspicious, incredible. She refuses to accept the official account and suspects that the death may be the result of a crime. Since she cannot bring Hale back to life, she attempts to save his integrity by discovering the truth about his death and making the criminals who killed him suffer. Her strength is in her resolve, expressed in her persistent questioning of those involved and in her attempts to convince them to come clean. Ida soon discovers, through her questioning, that she is struggling against small enemies. Some of them are petty criminals, while others are indifferent police officers. She does not care. Hers is a true, persistent courage. She knows what is right and wants to do it.

Ida's trust in the world is blunt, joyful, at times almost childish. After her courageous resolution to pursue the truth about Hale's death, "her heart beat faster to the refrain: it's exciting, it's fun, it's living."[7] Greene's description accords with my limited personal experience. If you act with true courage against small enemies while trusting the world, you'll soon discover that doing so is often exciting. Furthermore, struggling for what is right can, at times, be fun, because, frequently in such a struggle, you live fully—you're not letting life merely pass by. My experience also supports a theme repeatedly stressed by Greene: The indifference and passivity of simple people are sordid attitudes that allow evil to prevail.

Brown in *The Comedians* is another of Greene's unsung heroes who does not await great occasions. He despises the evil of Papa Doc Duvalier and considers his vile ministers and sycophantic aides despicable. Brown also hates the Tontons Macoute who instill terror in the poverty-stricken, economically exploited population of Haiti by their wicked, greedy, and brutal deeds. Brown never encounters Duvalier; he does meet a few of his ministers when he accompanies the presidential candidate, Smith, who wishes to set up a center of vegetarianism in the country. In these meetings, Brown is cordial, but he lets the ministers sense that he perceives their mendacity, their greed and lust for power, their bad faith, and their evil deeds. In subtle ways, he conveys to them that he despises such evils.

When he encounters the Tontons Macoute, Brown never blinks. Despite their concealing their eyes behind dark sunglasses, Brown faces up to them. By not blinking, he lets them know that he sees their blatant terror tactics for what they are—a manifestation of evil. Before these armed small enemies, who are callous, greedy, and wicked, who often viciously murder whoever stands in their way, Brown struggles not to let his fears show. Of course, in refusing to blink when confronted with the brutal terror of the Tontons Macoute, Brown is endangering his life. Is that not what being truly courageous means?

Brown trusts the world, through the persons he trusts: Joseph, Philipot, Doctor Magiot, Hamit, and Mr. and Mrs. Smith. He never attempts to manipulate these people or merely use them for his own needs. He readily shares the world, his experiences, and his concerns with them. This ability to share quite frequently helps Brown to reach worthy decisions in his own struggles.

~

In *It's a Battlefield*, Greene describes an array of characters from several segments of English society who lack simple courage and trust in the world. No detailed struggle of an unsung hero appears in this novel. Caroline Bury, who tries to save the life of the convicted bus driver, Drover, has simple courage and trust in the world. But she is ill and aging, perhaps on the verge of death, and she is very much on the periphery of the major events in the novel. Her unsuccessful attempts to bring politicians to act justly reveal that, by refusing even to consider the demands of justice, a large number of people in English society have become indifferent to many evils in their midst. Put differently, if we exclude Caroline Bury, all the characters described in *It's a Battlefield* are mediocre, bleak, uninspiring, and at times perverted and stupid; their insipid daily choices lead them to live a muddled, dismal, confined, and spiritually vacuous life. Simple courage and trust in the world are conspicuously lacking.

Beyond its condemnation of contemporary English society, *It's a Battlefield* discloses an important truth. Capitalism, which establishes society as a battlefield where each person is merely an individual struggling to survive and attain material benefits, very often leads to a total eradication of the simple courage and trust in the world that are necessary to a worthy life. London, as Greene describes it in this novel, is merely a Hobbesian battlefield where the "miserable condition of Warre" prevails and there is no place for things that are worthy in themselves. As early as the first page, the Assistant Commissioner, who is a major character, decides that justice is not his business. Slowly, one learns that the Assistant Commissioner's indifference to justice and to other worthy things, such as love or beauty, is hardly exceptional. The results are evident. In the bleak Hobbesian battlefield that the novel depicts, genuine friendship is almost impossible, generosity is very rare, and there is almost no place for even simple acts of heroism. Opportunism is considered the only way to thrive.

I have repeatedly emphasized that Greene's novels condemn indifference to the fate of the world and to the sufferings of other persons. In *It's a Battlefield* and in other novels, the reader quickly discerns that the Hobbesian battlefield embraced by capitalism is an area in which any person can bask in indifference. Even before capitalism reached its recent triumphs, Fyodor Dostoyevsky pointed out the insipidity of basking in indifference: "an indifferent man has no longer any faith at all, nothing but an ugly fear, and that only on rare occasions, if he is a sentimental man."[8]

What characterizes an individual who is struggling in a Hobbesian battlefield? Consider the lonely Assistant Commissioner. Survival, success in his job, and loyalty to the system that employs him are the only matters that he deems worthy of his attention. He almost never relates to or even considers his responsibility, as a moral person, for the fate of that part of the world that engages him. He has faith only in the system that employs him, and an ugly fear of what he will do with his life once he retires. Like Dostoyevsky, Greene shows that such an attitude of indifference stifles genuine human interaction and leads to a spiritually empty existence. There is a vicious circle here, however. Living a spiritually vacuous existence deepens the Assistant Commissioner's loneliness and solidifies his indifference, while his indifference supports his spiritual vacuity.

The conclusions stemming from *It's a Battlefield* merit repeating. The struggle for survival and success in a Hobbesian battlefield discourages the simple courage and trust in the world that characterize the lives and decisions of all of Greene's unsung heroes. Immersing oneself totally and wholeheartedly in this battlefield while accepting its inherent principles means developing an indifference to the world, to other people, and to things that are worthy in themselves, such as justice, love, or beauty. In short, living according to the dictates of a Hobbesian battlefield leads people to choose a mediocre, banal, and spiritually barren existence.

～

The whiskey priest in *The Power and the Glory* is perhaps Greene's most vivid example of a person who persistently rejects the evil of an oppressive, unjust regime with true courage and trust in the world. While constantly fleeing the law officials in a province in southern Mexico, where it has been decreed that priests are forbidden to conduct Catholic services and practicing priests are condemned to death, the whiskey priest holds services, hears confessions, baptizes children, and does whatever he can to help the people he meets observe their faith. His initial attitude toward those he encounters is to accept them as partners with whom he shares the world and to whom he entrusts his being. Of course, like D. in *The Confidential Agent*, the whiskey priest is wary, shrewd, vigilant, and on guard. He is unwilling to let the half-caste betray him to the army unit that is searching for him so as to obtain a 700-peso reward. He refuses to surrender to the authorities and to betray his calling and religious responsibilities. Nevertheless, the priest's wariness and shrewd responses when faced with danger never lead him to change his initial attitude of trust in the world.

Rose Cullen falls in love with D. and gallantly supports him in the fight against his evil enemies. The whiskey priest wanders alone, always alone, on mule or on foot, through the cities, towns, forests, meadows, and hamlets of the Mexican province where the Catholic Church has been outlawed. He is rejected by a woman with whom he once slept and fathered a girl, as well as by his daughter. But this woman shelters him, even while telling him never to return to their hamlet. He is respected by the poor and needy for whom he conducts services. These poor will never betray him, but they will not be living partners. The whiskey priest has no partners. The institution that had supported him, the Catholic Church, in which he might have found partners or colleagues, no longer exists in the province. All the other priests have fled. Throughout his travels the priest never encounters a person with whom he can share his anguish, his fears, his trials, or his travails. This aloneness, even while daily defying evil decrees and trusting simple people, contributes to the whiskey priest's glory.

Another important reason for the whiskey priest's glory is that he has true courage. He does not await great occasions. The possibility of waiting to act at what might be called a great occasion never crosses his mind. The priest often finds himself in dangerous situations, surrounded by people whom it might be wrong to trust, yet he always responds courageously to what the situation demands. The night he spends in a jail cell with dozens of other prisoners, among them petty criminals, during which he discloses that he is a priest, exemplifies his courageous responses. Greene seems to be indicating that, even though the whiskey priest is no spiritual luminary, his simple courage and trust in the world help him to bring some rays of the light of spirituality into the lives of those he encounters.

The Power and the Glory also seems to be suggesting that, in today's world, true glory belongs to those simple, courageous persons who, through their small daily deeds, challenge the prevailing, unjust, powerful regimes. Often these modest fighters against evil will fail and suffer. Some, like the whiskey priest, may be killed by representatives of a wicked regime. Yet, even from the title of the novel, it is evident that Greene does not believe that this failure mars the glory of such people.

From his other novels, from his personal and political writings, (such as *Getting to Know the General*), and from his many letters to editors of newspapers, it is evident that Greene considered most twentieth-century regimes unjust and often evil. In these writings, he describes and condemns many of the evils that a host of intellectuals have deemed acceptable in twentieth-century society, such as the French and American military involvement in Vietnam and other parts of Indochina. As this book indicates, I agree with Greene's assessment of the widespread evil that prevails. I should add, however, that for us simple people who wish, however partially, to challenge these evil regimes—regimes whose leaders are supported by many sophisticated academic sycophants and usually by their country's media—for us humble fighters against evil, the simple fortitude and trust in other people that the whiskey priest lives can be a source of strength and, at times, of inspiration.

～

The whiskey priest's life and death, like the struggles of D. and of Rose Cullen, point to an important spiritual message that can be found in other novels by Greene, such as *A Burnt-Out Case*. The lives of a few of Greene's unsung heroes indicate that the only way to live spiritually in this world, where evil very often prevails and is supported by powerful regimes, is through courage and trust in the world. Put differently, when aloneness, such as that of the whiskey priest, is coupled with simple courage and trust in the world, it is often transformed into a solitude that can become the womb of a spiritual life. When genuine dialogue and love emerge, as occurs between D. and Rose, thanks to their courage and their trust in the world, this dialogue and love can lead beyond their personal relation to a spiritually enhancing life.

These simple messages are hardly new. They are central to the lives and sayings of the Hebrew prophets. Indeed, the resounding sayings of Moses, Amos, Hosea, Jeremiah, Elijah, and the other Biblical prophets reveal their solitude, simple courage, trust in the world, and willingness to enter into dialogue in even the most adverse circumstances. It is no wonder that their engaging locutions and difficult struggles continue to guide many persons who seek to live a spiritual existence.

I concede wholeheartedly that Greene's unsung heroes are hardly comparable to the Hebrew prophets. No godly spirit rests upon these simple people and calls them to a mission that guides their lives. They are humble fellow human beings who have decided to challenge specific evils that they encounter and who have the courage to trust the world while fighting evil. Yet, there is a significant area in which these humble strugglers are comparable to the prophets—in their failures. Writing on the Bible, Martin Buber has pointed out, that, from Moses to David, to Elijah, to Jeremiah, to Jonah—indeed, in almost all its texts—the Bible glorifies failure, not success. Concerning the prophets, Buber added that the "glorification of failure [in the Bible] culminates in the long line of prophets whose existence is failure through and through. They live in failure; it is for them to fight and not to conquer."[9]

Greene's unsung heroes also live very often in failure. They, too, often fight but do not conquer. Think of Rose Cullen, D., Arthur Rowe, Doctor Magiot, Brown, and others. In those rare instances when they succeed and attain a small measure of power, they strive to use it for the good, for bringing about a better world in whatever area in which they are engaged.

The spirituality of these courageous fighters against evil is certainly much less embracing and much less profound than that of the Hebrew prophets. Yet their plodding humble attempts to fight evil, to trust the world, to bring about good, and to live a worthy existence can still be inspiring. I shall return to some of the many links between fighting evil, glory, and a spiritual existence in upcoming chapters.

NOTES

1. Graham Greene, *The Confidential Agent* (London: Penguin, 1971), 63.

2. Thomas Hobbes, *Leviathan* (London: Everyman's Library, 1914), 87.

3. Graham Greene, *The Comedians* (London: Penguin, 1967), 281.

4. Graham Greene, *The Ministry of Fear* (London: Penguin, 1973), 43.

5. Greene, *The Comedians*, 285–86.

6. The citation from Paul Nizan appears in the lengthy foreword that Jean-Paul Sartre wrote to a reissued edition of Nizan's book *Aden Arabie*. See Paul Nizan, *Aden Arabie*, trans. Joan Pinkham (New York: Columbia University Press, 1987), 38–39.

7. Graham Greene, *Brighton Rock* (London: Penguin, 1966), 37.

8. Fyodor Dostoyevsky, *The Possessed*, trans. Constance Garnett (New York: Fawcett, 1966), 415.

9. Martin Buber, *On the Bible* (New York: Schocken, 1968), 143.

7
Sensitivity to Horror

Compare two journalists described in Graham Greene's novels: Thomas Fowler in *The Quiet American* and Montagu Parkinson in *A Burnt-Out Case*. Thomas Fowler is sensitive to the horrors of the unjust colonial war in Vietnam, even though he recognizes that he can do very little to halt the evil and the agony. The reader soon becomes aware of Fowler's horror, as in his description of the killings and the suffering of the Vietnamese people in Phat Diem, during his flight in a bomber on active bombing duty over North Vietnam, or in his response to the explosion in central Saigon. Fowler is very much aware of the political evil of the French government and its allies, especially the United States. He knows that decisions by these governments are the source of much of the suffering, horror, and evil of this war of oppression. Furthermore, because he has the courage to be sensitive to horror, Fowler never becomes cynical.

In contrast, Montagu Parkinson has chosen an existence that is the epitome of cynicism. He has no sensitivity to the plight or concerns of any of the human beings whom he encounters. His sole desire and daily project is to write a story that will sell. For that, he plays with sentimentality. Note that much of the description of Montagu Parkinson also fits Mabel Warren in *Stamboul Train*; hence, Parkinson is not the only cynical, callous journalist in Greene's work. Producing a story that will sell justifies any means that Parkinson may choose. He packs his articles with mawkishness, lies, half truths, and unconfirmed rumors. Furthermore, Parkinson has no qualms when he strews personal ruin along the path of publishing a scoop; he could not care less about the sufferings of the people whom he encounters and whose stories he publishes. As long as the path leads to a story that will sell, Parkinson is satisfied. Need I add that Montagu Parkinson has chosen to be totally insensitive to horror and that he probably never sees evil?

The comparison between Fowler and Parkinson reveals the difference between an unsung hero and a cynical supporter of evil. Through his unsung heroes, Greene indicates that fighting evil very often begins with the horror that a person experiences when he or she perceives specific instances of evil. Experiencing horror is often lucid, direct, and immediate, as in Anna-Luise Fischer's horror at her father's repeated evil deeds, especially his wickedness toward her mother, in *Dr. Fischer of Geneva or The Bomb Party*. Another instance of someone immediately experiencing horror is Monsignor Quixote's courageous decision to halt forcefully the defiling of the church statue of Our Lady by the rich Mexicans, despite Sancho's warnings. And, of course, Fowler experiences immediate horror when he comprehends the results of the bomb that explodes in downtown Saigon, killing and maiming dozens of innocent people.

Anna-Luise does not reflect or deliberate; she sees the evil performed by her father for what it is and is horrified. The same holds true for Monsignor Quixote in his reaction to people pinning money on the statue of Our Lady and for Fowler when he comprehends the results of the bombing of Saigon that Pyle has helped to organize. Borrowing a term from Sartre, one can say that the horror experienced by Anna-Luise, by Monsignor Quixote, and by Thomas Fowler is pre-reflective. They see the terrible evil lucidly, without a need to define, conceptualize, explain, reflect, or deliberate. Evil exists here and now, and a person who has the courage to be sensitive to evil will comprehend it.

~

Do scholars who write about Greene's work relate to the experiencing of horror that is frequently described in his novels? Does their scholarship express the idea, often repeated in Greene's writings, that, today more than ever, people must be sensitive to horror, especially the horror of evil, if they are to retain their true humanity? From my descriptions of scholarly work on Greene in previous chapters, it should come as no surprise that, unfortunately, the answer to both questions is a resounding no!

Consider two additional examples, both short, book-length scholarly summaries of Greene's writings, one by John Spurling and the other by David Pryce-Jones.[1] Both books are titled *Graham Greene*. Though I will not present the general approach adopted by each of these studies, one similarity is evident. Evil in the world and horror at that evil are never discussed, nor is the need to fight evil ever brought up. In short, these scholars consider Greene's writings as works to be judged by so-called artistic criteria that seem to have nothing to do with the world in which we live. They never seem to wonder if the criteria for a good novel might be that it is a good story that both is true to life and illuminates aspects of human existence. Their writing does not ever mention the simple fact that, to be true to life in the twentieth century, as any sensitive and moral person will perceive, it is necessary to relate to the overwhelming presence of evil that arouses horror.

Let me briefly recall, with some slight variations, a theme mentioned in previous chapters. There is something both ludicrous and sad—indeed, inane—in a lengthy discussion of Greene's novels that does not mention evil and that does not disclose sensitivity to the horrors of evil. For fifty years and more, Graham Greene wrote novels that describe existing evils; again and again, he described instances of evil that arouse horror. In these novels, he also presented the lives of quite a few courageous unsung heroes who are sensitive to horror and who fight evil. I can only conclude that a scholar who overlooks this central theme of Greene's writing is condemning his or her scholarship to banality.

What is more, on any given day during the entire twentieth century, any person who cared about fellow human beings would have perceived terrible instances of evil that had recently occurred or were currently occurring, and which aroused horror. The genocidal massacres and ethnic cleansing that have taken place during the past few years in Bosnia and in Rwanda are striking examples. The same is true of the continuing brutal oppression and exploitation—since the beginning of the twentieth century and before—of the peoples of Central America by political thugs and death squads that are firmly supported, trained, and financed by the U.S. government. Such instances of terrible evils and horrors are here with us daily. We share the world with those who suffer these evils, as Greene's novels repeatedly show. Yet, both Spurling and Pryce-Jones write as if evil and horror do not exist, either in the novels of Graham Greene or in the world that we share with the evildoers and with the downtrodden and the oppressed. It is almost redundant to add that such scholarship is unworthy of Graham Greene.

~

Contemporary evil leaders know that sensitivity to horror frequently requires courage. Persons who experience horror may decide to fight the evil performed by these leaders—and to condemn them. Consequently, these leaders strive to extinguish the possibility of people experiencing horror when they encounter the evil and suffering that are a result of their deeds. They strive to desensitize people to the horrors of evil. One such desensitized person is Alden Pyle in The Quiet American; another is, of course, Montagu Parkinson. These two characters reveal that twentieth-century leaders and regimes have frequently succeeded in desensitizing many so-called "highly respected and successful citizens" to the horrors of evil that they have instigated. How is this done?

In other books, I have pointed out that many Western leaders employ large cohorts of academics who betray their commitment to truth and decide to be highly educated sycophants. The major task of these academic toadies is to find ways to desensitize large segments of the populace to the evil done by the regime that employs them.[2] An example of such desensitizing, which I have not fully elaborated in other writings, involves the spread of homelessness and poverty in the United States. One does not need to be endowed with keen insight to perceive that the growth in the horrible phenomenon of homelessness, of people who have no home in the world and must live in the streets, has rarely been discussed as a direct outcome of Ronald Reagan's evil policies—whether in the U.S. mainstream media, in the Congress, or among large segments of the so-called intellectual elite. Among these intellectuals and political leaders, the homeless may be mentioned, but they will be considered a natural phenomenon, like a snowstorm or a heat wave. Nothing can be done about it, except perhaps some minor steps to relieve visible suffering by, for instance, setting up overnight hostels.

Concerning recent U.S. government policies that have spread poverty while enriching the wealthy, Noam Chomsky has repeatedly pointed out the appalling results. Here are a few recent enlightening facts:

> in Manhattan the income gap between rich and poor is greater than in Guatemala, and within the U.S. is surpassed only by a group of 70 households in a former leper colony in Hawaii. . . . The great corporations [in the United States] are enjoying "dazzling" profits, *Fortune* magazine exults. . . . Meanwhile, the Census Bureau reports that 95 percent of the population has lost income since 1989, with a 7 percent decline in median family income continuing through the "Clinton Recovery."[3]

Unfortunately, Chomsky's writings on the horrors of evil in the United States are ignored by almost all intellectuals. If journalists in the mainstream media and most intellectuals in the United States ever read his writings, they will be quick to adopt what they call "an objective perspective." They will argue that one must view the current economic situation in the United States "nonjudgmentally." It would be much wiser to call their approach a desensitizing perspective that justifies government evil.

Why desensitizing? Because this perspective permits thousands of American intellectuals to disregard the facts that Chomsky presents and to see no evil in deliberate government policies that impoverish large segments of the population—millions of people, citizens of the United States—so that a few rich people can get much richer. As in the case of the homeless, these intellectuals and journalists attempt to convey the message that the deliberate deeds of Ronald Reagan, George Bush, Bill Clinton, and the Congress—deeds that led to the findings in the citation from Chomsky—are as inevitable as a hurricane on the East Coast. These horrible facts, they will falsely say, are merely a result of the way the market works or a result of significant democratic principles. They ignore Chomsky's factual arguments that prove the opposite: that deliberate government decisions led to the spread of the phenomenon of homelessness. Furthermore, horror at such injustice and at the degradation of human existence caused by creating millions of homeless individuals has vanished.

A second step in desensitizing the population requires redirecting the discussion. For instance, in the United States, readers, listeners, and viewers are repeatedly exposed to politicians and intellectuals who discuss the importance of welfare reform—as if that were the major problem that their government faces. By directing the attention of the populace elsewhere (for instance, to the supposed problem of welfare reform), persons learn not to experience horror when they encounter homeless people and beggars; they thus do not learn about widespread poverty. Let me say it again. The focusing of attention on a so-called general problem insidiously instructs people to overlook and to forget the plight of homeless people who are strewn in the streets from Manhattan to Berkeley, as well as the plundering of the public coffers by the wealthy. This tactic teaches people to be oblivious to governmental injustice and to the horrors of the poverty that is spreading in the United States.

As Greene shows, for both manners of desensitizing, journalists like Montagu Parkinson are valuable. Parkinson describes evil or good as almost inevitable. In addition, his writing directs the attention of his readers away from, say, the gross and ruinous insensitivity of fanatics like Rycker, whose vile deeds are evident to whoever is willing to see evil. The reason is obvious. Parkinson wants to entertain his readers, not to convey a truth to them or to confront them with a problem that may demand thinking. His bizarre, often inane style expresses this quest for superficiality and banality. He appeals to the lowest common denominator among his readers, using the most popular and worn-down cliches. His writing intends to appeal to sentiment; it does not demand thinking.

The opportunities and way of life that face both Fowler and Parkinson emphasize a major point made by Chomsky.[4] The subservient media in democracies help evil politicians desensitize the public to the horrors of the evil that they have done. When Fowler wants to write minor hints that will partially expose the horrors that he witnesses in the ongoing war in Vietnam, he is certain that his report will not pass the French censor. Even if, by devious means, he succeeds in evading the censor, his editor in Britain will hardly ever print the horrors that Fowler could describe. In short, the horrors that Fowler witnesses are effaced from history by censors and by the editorial policies of the mainstream media.

By portraying Fowler's and Parkinson's choices and way of life, Greene is presenting a poignant message. In the mainstream media of the United States, France, Britain, and other Western democracies, clear and honest writing that poignantly describes the horrors and the evils that result from the policies of their governments has well nigh disappeared. The mendacious writing and shallow style of callous people like Montagu Parkinson has pretty much triumphed.

All of Greene's unsung heroes are sensitive to the horrors of the evil they encounter. This experiencing of horror is linked to a belief that they express through deeds. One can formulate the belief thus: We share the world with others; and so it is our responsibility to diminish the suffering and protect the lives and integrity of these others. Note that this belief, which guides their decisions, is seldom expressed in words.

Anne Crowder in A Gun for Sale is recognized as a heroine at the end of the book. Hence, she is not a typical unsung hero, though one might speculate that her fame will fade rapidly. Anne decides to get involved with the wicked Mr. Davis-Cholmondely when she perceives the fears of the silent crowd watching the portentous news of an upcoming disaster being broadcast on electric bulbs; the news describes England moving toward an imminent European war. Anne has no memories of previous wars. Through her sensitivity to the fears of the crowd, however, she becomes aware of the horror of war, and she fears the dangers that the war might bring to her love for Jimmy Mather. She knows she may have a slight chance to halt the war if she gets at the truth by getting to know Mr. Davis-Cholmondely better. Her response is courageous, of course. It is a decision to attempt to save her love and to protect the lives and integrity of her compatriots.

Anne Crowder is a simple example, some may say. What about the hotelier, Brown, in *The Comedians*? Granted that Brown perceives the horrors instigated by Papa Doc Duvalier and the Tontons Macoute, and he firmly rejects their evil deeds. Yet nowhere does he express a belief that we share the world with others or that it is our responsibility to protect their lives and integrity. After all, Brown himself was quite a swindler when, in Britain, he sold fake new-masters paintings to a mediocre aspiring elite. Is not the experiencing of horror, in the case of Brown, an example that counters the above statement about Greene's unsung heroes? And, in general, what is horror?

The Random House Dictionary defines horror as "an overwhelming and painful feeling caused by something frightfully shocking, terrifying, or revolting; a shuddering fear." I agree with this definition, yet two points must be added, which relate to horror at witnessing evil. When horror arises, it is very often linked to the sad plight of fellow human beings. As mentioned, many people recently experienced horror when they learned of the brutal, genocidal killings of more than half a million members of the Tutsi tribe in Rwanda. There are still many people in the United States who experience horror when they see homeless people strewn about the streets and read about the spread of poverty and homelessness. Consequently, and this is the second point, horror at an evil can arise only for persons who have adopted a way of life in which sharing the world with others and responsibility for these others is central to their being-in-the-world. Already in *Heart of Darkness*, Joseph Conrad poignantly depicted the ontological roots of horror when witnessing evil; he also indicated how rare a sharing and responsible way of life is in our age, which is dominated by a brutal capitalism, where the relentless pursuit of greed is a legitimate, dominant way of life and a major theme in human interaction.

Doctor Magiot correctly senses that Brown's decision to experience the horror that he encounters in Haiti is a responsible act. It testifies that Brown has been a sharing, responsible person, even if he may have acted dishonestly in the "painting business" that he set up in the past. His sharing and his assuming responsibility appear in many seemingly minor deeds throughout the book, such as his warmly helping Mr. and Mrs. Smith and his assisting Major Jones when he flees. Brown is a simple person. He is an unsung hero whose genuine acts of sharing and personal responsibility, together with his experiencing horror, reveal his sensitivity and courage.

~

It is early morning, before dawn. The extravagant evening party of corrupt officials, foreign consuls, smugglers, and top crooks is almost over. Wordsworth, Aunt Augusta's black African lover in *Travels with my Aunt* has been shot dead by a guard engaged by her racketeer and fugitive male companion, Mr. Visconti. His body is lying in the spacious garden surrounding the old mansion in Asunción, Paraguay, that Aunt Augusta has purchased for Mr. Visconti and herself. She hears of Wordsworth's death from her son, Henry Pulling, but continues to dance with Visconti, happily swirling to the final tune played by the orchestra.

At age seventy-five, Aunt Augusta could not care less about Wordsworth, who, in addition to loving her deeply, has helped her quite a bit during the past months and years. His death does not disturb or even slightly diminish her joy at living with a lover from her younger days, the swindler, fascist, and war-criminal Visconti. She happily sets up with him an illegal smuggling business based in Paraguay. Greene clearly shows that, throughout her life, Aunt Augusta has chosen to be desensitized to people who no longer bring her pleasure or who cannot be utilized for her immediate needs or pleasures. As her callous response to Wordsworth's death reveals, she seems never to experience horror.

Note, however, that she is very sentimental, caring very much about her past and present feelings, as well as about the importance of her stories. Indeed, Aunt Augusta well fulfills Dostoyevsky's observation that an evil person can be at once wicked and sentimental.[5] The distinction between sensitivity and sentimentality is quite evident. The sensitive person cares for others and for the world that he or she shares with these others; the sentimental person focuses on his or her own feelings. Thus, like Aunt Augusta, a sentimental person can be totally insensitive to the horrors of evil that confront him or her.

Is Aunt Augusta exceptional in her responses? Not at all. Today, in the heyday of a triumphant corporate capitalism, many people warmly embrace the tenets that guide Aunt Augusta: Other people exist solely as either a source of pleasure for me or a means to satisfy my needs.

I want to emphasize this point. Quite a few of Greene's novels, such as It's a Battlefield, Stamboul Train, The Captain and the Enemy, and England Made Me, clearly indicate that Aunt Augusta's principles underlie the worldview and the daily deeds of many people who adhere to the tenets of contemporary capitalism. These principles and deeds are also accepted by government officials. Indeed, it is hardly a secret that succeeding in a capitalist-oriented society usually means adhering to Aunt Augusta's vile, egotistical principles and her indifference to evil and horror.

Greene shows that, since the principles that Aunt Augusta and contemporary capitalism have chosen to live by are harsh and immoral, people frequently must be seduced to embrace them. I have already mentioned Aunt Augusta's seductive powers. For instance, her storytelling is not a genuine sharing of her past life; instead she relates stories so as to subjugate the bored Henry Pulling slowly to her will. Put succinctly, storytelling for Aunt Augusta is one of her means of seducing Henry Pulling to participate in her evil endeavors. It is a manner of changing an evil or mediocre deed into an interesting event or perhaps an entertaining adventure. Aunt Augusta does not believe in sharing—she believes only in seducing and in being seduced!

From the weaknesses and, yes, the boring stupidity of Henry Pulling, the reader learns that to fight evil you must firmly reject the ploys that evildoers use to seduce you to overlook their wickedness. You must always remember that evildoers are clever. In many books, Greene indicates that one major way of rejecting such seductions is to retain a sensitivity to horror. Through his boring, sedated, rather cowardly life as a bank clerk who is slowly promoted to become the manager of a local branch, Pulling has lost almost all sensitivity to what he meets in the world, including his sensitivity to horror. He is easy prey for Aunt Augusta.

~

Sensitivity to horror requires that you experience horror at evil deeds that you have instigated, if you did evil. I have already mentioned Conrad's *Heart of Darkness*, as teaching us much about experiencing horror. The scene in which Kurtz, on his deathbed and probably comprehending in retrospect his life and deeds, whispers "a cry that was no more than a breath: 'The horror! The horror!' " is also instructive.[6] These are Kurtz's last words. Conrad does not describe how Kurtz has lived with his horror, either during the few moments before he expires, or during the years that he has lived in Africa. Yet Conrad does consider Kurtz's seeing the horror before his death as a triumph of human courage and sensitivity.

By contrast, Graham Greene does describe the lives and the obstacles encountered by two persons who live with the horror of their own evil deeds: Arthur Rowe in *The Ministry of Fear* and Querry in *A Burnt-Out Case*. Overcome by guilt and steeped in repugnance at the horror of their actions, both Rowe and Querry attempt to flee. Rowe flees into a self-imposed solitude in which he endeavors to live alone with his crime—poisoning his wife who was slowly dying from an incurable disease. Rowe fears to trust other people and the world. Querry flees to a leper colony in the midst of Africa, as far away as possible from the ruinous and wicked way of life that he pursued and that was partially a result of his worldwide acclaim and success as an architect. Their flights fail. In both novels, Greene indicates that a sensitive person will find it difficult to flee the horror of his or her past. One must learn to live with this horror, Greene seems to be saying, and the best way to live with past evil actions is by trusting the world, which means trusting specific persons in the world.

Through the story of Arthur Rowe, Greene also shows that sensitivity to the horror of one's own evil deed can lead a person to fight evil. These instances may be rare, but they exist. Of course, if the evil a person has done is horrendous, such as the wicked deeds of Conrad's Kurtz, who uses savage methods to obtain ivory and who adorns the poles surrounding his hut with human heads, a metamorphosis into a fighter against evil may be impossible.

~

Let me say it once again: Greene's repeatedly showing us the importance of being sensitive to the horror of evil is bracing, refreshing, and quite exceptional in contemporary literature. Through his unsung heroes, he describes the possibility of a personally enhancing circle of choices. Sensitivity to horror requires choosing to live courageously and with lucidity; conversely, a courageous, lucid person is usually sensitive to horror. Furthermore, courage, lucidity, and sensitivity to horror are necessary to seeing the truth and, as suggested later in this study, to attaining wisdom.

Some may ask: Why is the linking of courage, lucidity, and sensitivity to horror and truth, as Greene presents it in the lives of his unsung heroes, so rare in contemporary fiction? I do not know. A full answer would probably require writing another book. One probable reason may be rooted in the comparison between Thomas Fowler and Montagu Parkinson that opens this chapter. Novelists may have learned that describing the horrors of prevailing evils and pointing a finger at the evildoers is quite frequently a slap in the face of the mainstream media, a condemnation of the evil corporations and the wicked politicians whom the mainstream media very often support. Such writing may be blocked by these powerful corporations and their intellectual sycophants.

In closing, let us imagine a reader of *The Comedians* who genuinely cares about fellow human beings. Papa Doc Duvalier's guilt is evident, as are many of the horrors he inflicted upon probably hundreds of thousands of innocent citizens and residents of Haiti. The support of the U.S. government and of the Western mainstream media for Duvalier's rampant wickedness and the despicable horrors of his regime is also evident. The caring reader learns that Papa Doc Duvalier, the politicians, and media of the United States all deserve to be condemned forcefully, wholeheartedly, and without mincing words. Thus, reading *The Comedians*, *The Quiet American*, or other of Greene's novels can be an educational experience, as to both the specific horrors and evils instigated, supported, and covered up by the Western powers and the importance of being sensitive to horror. It can also be a call to join those few persons who do attempt to halt the many evils that prevail.

It can be such a call because Greene's unsung heroes show the caring reader another important fact: It is possible for us simple persons, who are sensitive to the horrors of evil that we encounter, to attempt to do something to stop that evil. Greene also indicates that this sensitivity may frequently lead to depression, to a wish to flee, to a feeling of impotence, to rage. Nevertheless, as his novels show, without sensitivity to horror, a person loses his or her dignity, integrity, and the possibility of relating spiritually. Indeed, the sensitivity to horror of some of Greene's unsung heroes is a key to their integrity, dignity, and search for spiritual-ity—however vague, difficult, and challenging this search may be.

NOTES

1. John Spurling, *Graham Greene* (London: Methuen, 1983); David Pryce-Jones, *Graham Greene* (Edinburgh: Oliver and Boyd, 1963).

2. Haim Gordon, *Quicksand: Israel, the Intifada, and the Rise of Political Evil in Democracies* (East Lansing: Michigan State University Press, 1995). See also: Haim Gordon and Rivca Gordon, *Sartre and Evil: Guidelines for a Struggle* (Westport, CT: Greenwood Press, 1995).

3. Noam Chomsky, "Rollback II: 'Civilization' Marches On," *Z Magazine* 8: 2 (February 1995), 22.

4. Many of Noam Chomsky's writings make this point. See, for instance, Noam Chomsky, *World Orders, Old and New* (London: Pluto, 1994).

5. Fyodor Dostoyevsky, *The Brothers Karamazov*, trans. Richard Pevear and Larissa Volokhonsky (New York: Vintage, 1991), 25.

6. Joseph Conrad, *Heart of Darkness & The Secret Sharer* (New York: Signet, 1980), 147.

8
Failure and Integrity

One person fails woefully in *Stamboul Train*: Dr. Czinner. He is the only person who tries to fight evil. He attains integrity through his deeds. The reader will probably respond with pity, apathy, or revulsion to almost all the other characters in the novel, for Carleton Myatt, Mabel Warren, and no other characters make choices that lead to a life of integrity.

There is no necessary linkage between failing and attaining integrity, either in life or in Greene's novels. Richard Nixon failed to cover up his deceit in the Watergate case and lost all integrity, even though the docile mainstream press in the United States tried to revive his significance as a political pundit a bit before his death and printed laudatory eulogies after he expired. (As mentioned in previous chapters, the mainstream media rarely considered Nixon's many evil deeds in Southeast Asia worth condemning, nor did they suggest that these crimes were a reason for Nixon to lose respect or integrity.) Scobie in *The Heart of the Matter* is a seemingly good person who makes wrong decisions, fails flagrantly in his personal life, and loses his integrity.

There is also the possibility of retaining integrity while succeeding, as happens to Anne Crowder in *A Gun for Sale*. Nelson Mandela and Martin Luther King, Jr. succeeded in partially diminishing the blatant and brutal oppression of black Africans in South Africa and of African Americans in the United States; through persisting in their long struggles for justice, they both attained integrity. Like Dr. Czinner and other unsung heroes that Greene describes, however, those persons who fight evil very often fail. Yet they attract us because their integrity shines through their conspicuous, sad failures. This shimmer of integrity is frequently their only source of glory.

~

Someone may ask, What do you mean by integrity? Are you arguing that Aunt Augusta lacks integrity while Monsignor Quixote attains it? Aren't you fitting the word to your needs? In answer, here is *The Random House Dictionary* definition of integrity: "adherence to moral and ethical principles; soundness of moral character; honesty."

To add a live dimension to this definition, here is a description of a family that has attained integrity (from the autobiography of Alexander Herzen): "They had lately returned from [exile in] Siberia; they were ruined, yet they bore the stamp of dignity which calamity engraves, not on every sufferer, but on those who have borne misfortune with courage."[1]

The dictionary does not mention that a life of integrity is the result of certain basic choices. The citation from Herzen points to the most important of these choices. It is the decision to confront one's situation, including one's misfortunes, courageously. This means often confronting other people over matters of principle, about things that are worthy in themselves, such as truth, justice, love, beauty, or faith. As I have shown at length in other books, confrontation often means assuming responsibility for the situation in which I find myself; it is crucial for genuine dialogue, as well as for relating to truth and to other things that are worthy in themselves. A person's decision to confront other people on matters of principle or for things that are worthy means being willing to be confronted oneself on such matters.[2]

As already mentioned, Major Henry Scobie is a flagrant failure in his personal life. Because he persistently chooses to evade confrontations on matters of principle, Scobie has ruined his career, made irresponsible decisions, and gradually effaced his integrity. Greene shows that the soundness of Scobie's moral character has eroded slowly, often through minor, cowardly decisions in seamy matters. The decisions are cowardly because Scobie relentlessly seeks to evade confronting people, especially his wife Louise, but also his mistress Helen, the security officer Wilson, and the corrupt merchant Yusef. Greene also shows how, through minor cowardly decisions, step by step, the little dignity that Scobie has obtained in his honest service vanishes from his brow. Put differently, Scobie's cowardice when faced with rather minor personal calamities is what prevents him from obtaining the stamp of dignity that Herzen mentions.

Together with his persistent shrinking away from confrontation, Scobie expresses a deep pity for others. Greene shows, however, here and in other novels, that pity born of cowardice is very often ruinous, both to the person who pities and to those who are pitied. As Sartre indicates, pity is a passive activity, in which the person who pities does not initiate action but is carried along by events. Scobie's pity is indeed a passive activity. His nurturing of pity helps him to justify his flight from confrontations and from taking courageous stances, among them his not confronting Louise with the simple truth that he does not love her at all.

My brief portrayal of Scobie's ruinous decisions may seem much too simple. Greene hints that certain tenets of Catholicism encourage Scobie to choose pity over confrontation. But that is the point! Scobie flees from confrontation; in the process, he develops a distorted relation to religion that helps him to justify his flight. Unfortunately, most commentators who discuss Scobie's distorted religious faith do not perceive that truthful confrontation and genuine dialogue are manners of not sinking into the morass that Scobie has created for himself. Consider a few sentences, written by A. A. DeVitis, that summarize Scobie's religious beliefs in relation to his suicide.

> He [Scobie] does not so much fear hellfire as he does the permanent sense of loss of God that the Church teaches as a condition of hell. To be deprived of the God he loves is the worst torment of all for Scobie, yet he chooses this over giving more hurt to Louise and Helen. Sentimentally, he sees himself as Christ committing suicide for mankind.[3]

DeVitis understands that Scobie's pity is ruinous, his choice of suicide wrong, his Catholic faith quite distorted, and his sentimentality destructive. Yet he never mentions that confronting Louise and others with truths and on matters of principle might lead Scobie to a different existence—an existence that eschews ruinous pity or destructive sentimentality. Similarly, no other commentator on Scobie whom I have read suggests that confronting others—in the manner that Dr. Czinner boldly confronts his Yugoslavian judges—is an honest manner of sharing the world with others while living with integrity. They do not suggest that pity, for Scobie, is a manner of distancing himself from his fellow human beings. Likewise, no commentator mentions the slow, steady erosion of integrity that accompanies Scobie's flight from confrontations into a ruinous pity.

In Greene's novels, Scobie is not alone in fleeing truthful confrontations. Henry Pulling, in *Travels with my Aunt*, dares not confront Aunt Augusta on almost any topic. He never dares criticize her many immoral decisions and criminal deeds. The fact that Aunt Augusta is seductive merely strengthens my point. Many seductions, which seemingly justify not confronting issues or the people who do evil, encompass us daily. Living a worthy life means rejecting these seductions. But Henry Pulling flees from confrontation; again and again, he chooses not to reject his aunt's seductions. By his cowardly decisions, he is slowly pulled into the life of evil that Aunt Augusta has chosen to initiate and perform. The novel ends with Pulling having fully adapted himself to the life of a smuggler; the possibility of adhering to moral and ethical principles has disappeared from his life.

Another example of a person who flees from confrontation is Mr. Steiner in *Dr. Fischer of Geneva or The Bomb Party*. For many years after Dr. Fischer ruined his life, Steiner did not have the courage to confront Dr. Fischer and to brand him as evil. Steiner knew very well that Dr. Fischer destroyed his life and his love for Madame Fischer. He also knew that Dr. Fischer's cruel actions led to his wife's swift demise. Yet he was silent. Years later, Steiner finally decides to confront Dr. Fischer a moment before the latter shoots himself. During his many years of silence, Mr. Steiner suffered from his own cowardice, from his acceptance of the wickedness of Dr. Fischer, from his viewing Dr. Fischer as if he were as omnipotent as God Almighty. Need I add that neither Henry Pulling nor Mr. Steiner is a person who has attained integrity?

∾

Greene's unsung heroes do not fear confronting the evildoers and pointing out their evil to them. Very often this confrontation is dismissed by the evildoer as irrelevant and unworthy of response. Still, by confronting evil, the unsung hero adheres to moral principles and adds to his or her integrity. Look at a few examples.

At the end of *The Quiet American*, Fowler repeatedly confronts Pyle and strives to explain a simple principle: The indiscriminate bombing, killing, and mauling of innocent Vietnamese so as to serve the future interests of the United States is wrong and wicked. With a smile of innocence, Pyle brushes off this principle as puny and inconsequential. For Pyle, the quiet American, the lives of simple Vietnamese are dispensable, so long as his activities lead to attaining the political and economical objectives of the United States. Fowler fails to convince Pyle, and so he signals to the communists to kill him. Participation in this murder does not diminish Fowler's integrity.

Why? Fowler is sensitive to other persons and to the horror of evil; he pursues truth and even wisdom. He admits to having had neurotic hang-ups and some moments of cowardice, especially in his relations with women. Still, in his daily interactions, he adheres quite closely to Immanuel Kant's categorical imperative: "So act as if your maxims had to serve at the same time as a universal law."[4] One could quite easily argue, on Kantian grounds, that it is a moral act to murder a CIA agent who endorses and helps to instigate the mass killing and mauling of innocent people so as to further the future interests—specifically the economic interests—of his country. Put differently, a universal law could be formulated that protects innocent people from mass murderers, including those who murder innocent people so as to further the interests of their country, even if such protection requires killing the mass murderer. Furthermore, Fowler is lucid and basically honest; very little bad faith informs his existence.

Does his death, which is a failure of sorts, endow Pyle with integrity? Not at all! Pyle is insensitive, dense, and quite stupid. By donning the mask of innocence, he flees confrontations, especially confrontations on matters of principle. Note also that Pyle adheres to no universal moral principles; perhaps the closest he comes to such a principle is that fair play should exist between white men. Pyle is not at all interested in truth or knowledge, especially concerning what is happening in Vietnam, nor does he make any attempt to be lucid or to counter bad faith. As Greene indicates, Pyle's armor against Fowler's confrontations is made up of his choice of ignorance and his seemingly good intentions—intentions that serve an evil regime and that have nothing to do with moral principles. Small wonder that Pyle is not a person of integrity.

∼

Toward the end of *Brighton Rock*, Ida confronts Rose with the truth about Pinkie. He is a murderer who has killed two men, and he will soon try to eliminate her. Rose is adamant. She forcefully resists Ida's attempts to engage in dialogue, even though she senses, albeit vaguely, that Ida is right. Rose recognizes that trusting Pinkie is dangerous; her life and future are at stake. Still, Ida's pleading and her knowledge of the truth are shrugged off, discarded.

In trying to convince Rose, Ida fails. Nevertheless, her struggle for what is right and against a brutal murderer is worthy. As I have repeatedly mentioned, many Greene scholars do not appreciate Ida's struggle, nor do they perceive her integrity;

adding to the list of myopic writers and their inane attempts to discredit Ida will bring little additional knowledge or wisdom.[5] Rather, I want to digress and to reject the ontology underlying most attempts to belittle or ignore Ida's worthy deeds, which include her saving Rose's life and stopping Pinkie's murdering spree. Such a digression will help to clarify why Ida attains integrity.

To discredit Ida and to minimize the integrity of her deeds, many scholars who write about Greene's novels suggest that there is an almost unbridgeable cleavage between right and wrong, on the one hand, and good and evil, on the other. Right and wrong, these scholars claim, pertain to our everyday deeds and actions in the secular world, while good and evil relate to the religious realm, to the eternal life promised to Catholics by the Church of Rome and perhaps to their adherents by other religions.

The problem with this distinction is that to give it an ontological basis, you have to accept some form of Manicheism—to admit that evil has a being of its own that is at a different pole from the being of good. This existing pole of evil is what struggles against the good, and we are merely its pawns in the game or struggle. Let me repeat. To justify ontologically the distinction between good and evil on the one hand, and right and wrong on the other, one must accept some version of Manicheism. Because if evil exists but has nothing to do with wrong or wicked deeds—deeds like Pinkie's killing Hale or his manipulating Rose into marrying him, even though he despises her—if evil is not a concept that expresses what is common in these deeds, then evil must have a being of its own.

It is hardly a secret that, for quite a few centuries, the ontology of Manicheism has been rejected by an overwhelming majority of Western religious philosophers, theologians, and Biblical scholars. Put briefly, all of these thinkers believe that evil exists but that it has what may be called a borrowed existence. Evil has no being of its own. Satan is merely a figment of the imagination, a legend.

Evil, the non-Manichean believes, is our way of defining the deeds of persons who have turned away from the good—for instance, the wicked deeds of Pinkie Brown or of Alden Pyle, which destroy the freedom of other human beings. On a broader canvas, the cruel deeds of fascists who have destroyed the freedom of their fellow human beings or the brutal deeds of robbers who have not followed the precepts of the Decalogue are evil. Indeed, all those who reject Manicheism believe that evil exists only in evil deeds, like Cain's murder of Abel, which are the results of people deciding to do wrong and fulfilling their decision. Hence, there is no cleavage between right and wrong and good and evil. If, as these thinkers hold, there is no such cleavage between right and wrong and good and evil, then Greene scholars who play with these concepts are either Manicheans or ontologically establishing a pseudo-problem.

Furthermore, in no case do these Greene scholars give any justifications for adopting their Manichean approach; in no instance do they suggest what allows them to attribute being to evil. They write as if evil has being, without examining their thesis. One wonders: Did they ever read contemporary theology or philosophy? It is therefore hardly strange that these scholars do not admit that by doing right, as Ida does, a person adheres to moral principles and obtains integrity.

I submit that there has been a fascinating attempt to accept a partial cleavage between right and wrong and good and evil in Søren Kierkegaard's *Fear and Trembling*.[6] Yet it is precisely *Fear and Trembling* that reveals another aspect of the shallow thinking of those scholars who discuss Greene's novels and have suggested that there exists a cleavage between right and wrong and good and evil in our everyday lives.

Kierkegaard believes that the patriarch Abraham's decision to fulfill God's command and to sacrifice his son Isaac, as described in Genesis 22, requires a teleological suspension of the ethical. Kierkegaard explains that this suspension is necessary for Abraham to commit an act of absolute faith in response to a command by an absolute God. This terrifying act makes Abraham into a knight of faith; yet, Kierkegaard indicates, because Abraham does transcend the realm of the ethical, he is incomprehensible to us. The depth of Abraham's faith in God is almost inconceivable, according to Kierkegaard. Still we must admit that this faith guides Abraham to do something that is at once ethically wrong and yet very worthy. In brief, Kierkegaard indicates, through his ethically wrong deed, Abraham transcends the ethical realm and enters the religious realm.

Certainly, as the continuing scholarly discussion of *Fear and Trembling* reveals, there are quite a few philosophical and theological problems in Kierkegaard's presentation of Abraham's teleological suspension of the ethical, but I shall not touch upon them. Let me instead make a minor point. None of Graham Greene's evil characters ever stands in a situation that bears any resemblance to the situation of Abraham: not Pinkie, Aunt Augusta, Erik Krough, Major Scobie, Alden Pyle, Andre Rycker, Montagu Parkinson, or any other evildoer in Greene's novels. Not one of them hears a command from God or one of His prophets. The closest example I can think of in Greene's writing that faintly resembles Kierkegaard's teleological suspension of the ethical occurs in *The End of the Affair*. In this novel, Sarah gives up her love for Bendrix because of a vow to God. Yet there is something of caricature in Greene's presentation of Sarah. Her fulfilling of her vow and her discarding the blessing and joy of love do not make her a person of integrity. Moreover, she acts in a cowardly way when she avoids meeting Bendrix and confiding her vow to him. I should perhaps add that no person who fights evil emerges in this novel, which is why I have not mentioned it until now.

An unsung hero whose acts very partially resemble Kierkegaard's Abraham is the whiskey priest in *The Power and the Glory*, especially when he sacrifices his life to hear the confession of a murderer. The sacrifice may have been wrong from an ethical perspective, yet one can argue that it propels the whiskey priest into the sanctity of religious martyrism. Note, however, that the priest firmly believes that, in returning to hear the confession, he is doing what is right. This choice adds to his integrity.

I can only conclude that the cleavage between right and wrong and good and evil that scholars have attempted to attribute to Greene's description of existence is itself wrong and morally ruinous. As I have shown in great detail, Greene's ontology is down to earth; it has no links to Manicheism. Similarly, Greene's writings do not describe at length exercises of consciousness that faintly resemble those depicted in *Fear and Trembling*. No knights of faith appear in his novels. The people who attain integrity are sinners, like the whiskey priest, like Ida, Brown, and Fowler, who strive to do the right thing in a world where much evil prevails.

We again reach a conclusion mentioned previously. The myopia of scholars who refuse to see the linkage in Greene's novels between doing right and bringing about good seems to be more than a flagrant misreading. It seems to be a flight from assuming responsibility for the fate of the world. Small wonder, therefore, that these scholars often refuse to see the connection between the unsung heroes' frequent failures in fighting evil and their attaining integrity.

~

Aunt Augusta has no stories to tell that suggest that she has attained integrity. She cannot have such stories, for her deeds are immoral. Similarly, Eric Krough, in *England Made Me*, does not attain integrity, nor does Dr. Fischer. Yet these cruel immoral people, who, in Herzen's words, bear no stamp of dignity, are honored by the so-called elites of their society—Aunt Augusta in Paraguay, Erik Krough in Sweden, and Dr. Fischer in Geneva and all of Switzerland. By contrast, Greene's unsung heroes are rarely honored by the elites of their society. Indeed, a few of these heroes are viewed by those who meet them as somewhat eccentric. Think of Ida, Brown, or Dr. Czinner. Others may be considered struggling or disillusioned idealists, such as Doctor Magiot in *The Comedians*, the whiskey priest in *The Power and the Glory*, or perhaps, for a short while, Anne Crowder and Thomas Fowler. To judge by Greene's novels, being honored by the so-called elite of one's society very rarely coincides with attaining personal integrity.

What sort of people does the elite of contemporary society honor? Not people whose daily deeds are guided by adherence to moral or ethical principles, or those whose soundness of moral character shines. Greene shows that the people honored in contemporary capitalist society are the wealthy and those in power who faithfully serve the wealthy. He also shows that these honored people are usually very boring: Their lives are shallow, insipid, and very often immoral and corrupt. If you open a newspaper you will find that the so-called friends of Dr. Fischer in *Dr. Fischer of Geneva or The Bomb Party*, the Toads, are pretty much an example of the wealthy people whom capitalist societies honor.

Aunt Augusta is no exception. She is mean and often evil, yet she develops a seductiveness that partially conceals her meanness and helps her to flee boredom. In Paraguay, she is honored for her money and her success in setting up a smuggling company. Paraguay's miniscule capitalist society honors money and financial success, even when they are attained by criminal acts. In most instances, capitalist societies do not care if such success is attained through deceit, brutal exploitation, and cruel oppression, as is often done by contemporary corporations in the major capitalist countries. Look again at Erik Krough. He is greatly honored in Sweden solely because of his financial success. Nothing in his personality is attractive. He has no interesting ideas or creative thoughts. He has done nothing worthy for his fellow human beings. He is spiritually infantile.

Erik Krough is hardly an exception. I have already mentioned that many leaders, such as Ronald Reagan and Margaret Thatcher, who are honored in the West, resemble Krough. I am definitely not being facetious when I present the notion that the capitalist elite of Japanese society also resembles a bunch of Erik Kroughs. Let us play a bit with this thought, since it reveals the spiritual infantility that comes to prevail when an entire society fervently embraces the so-called blessings of corporate capitalism. It also reveals what happens when a society—almost all its members—ostensibly eschews adherence to the moral and ethical principles needed to live a life of integrity.

Japan is greatly honored among nations, all too often because of the country's industrial and financial success and its resulting great wealth. Like the vapid and vile life of Erik Krough, however, spiritual life in Japan today is virtually nonexistent. Worthy studies in philosophy, good literature, great music, great art, the pursuit of wisdom or justice, care for the world and its environment, attempts to attain equality for women, respect for the freedom and human rights of other persons—none of these can be found in contemporary Japan, unless, perhaps, one seeks at the extreme fringes. At these fringes one will also find a small minority of organizations contesting the hegemonic situation that prevails and is accepted by most Japanese. The influence of these organizations upon life in Japan is almost nil.

In addition, few Japanese have more than a very limited understanding of their basic freedoms. Consider the attitude of Japanese citizens toward laws:

> nothing in their history encourages ordinary Japanese citizens to think that the law exists to protect them. Never adding up to a system based on rational, philosophical principles of justice, traditional Japanese law consisted of little more than lists of commands to be blindly obeyed by commoners. . . . On the whole, Japanese still think of law as an instrument of constraint used by the government to impose its will. Japanese officials are free to pick and choose among laws, using them to further their own causes.[7]

On the basis of this citation, it is fair, therefore, to ask if a genuine quest for things that are worthy in themselves, such as justice, exists anywhere in Japan? As mentioned, on the remote sidelines of elite society or in small minority movements, one can probably find something resembling such a quest. Karel van Wolferin, from whose book the above citation is taken, does not mention encountering such a quest during the decades he lived in Japan and studied its society. The citation reveals merely one of many areas in which, as Wolferin shows, Japanese society is spiritually infantile. Note that Greene suggests—through his portrayal of Erik Krough and also through his depiction of Sir Marcus and Mr. Davis in A Gun for Sale—that such spiritual infantility is characteristic of almost all persons who constitute the elite of capitalism.

Wolferin's well-documented book also reveals that Japanese spiritual infantility accords very well with the neo-fascist political regime that reigns unmolested. He shows that Japan, which, as already mentioned, is greatly honored in our capitalist-run world, has offered the world nothing beyond a broad array of seductive consumer goods and new, alluring methods of manipulating people. Moral integrity and spirituality are conspicuously lacking in Japan and also in all its interactions with other nations.

A well-known example is worth repeating. Japanese statesmen and many ordinary citizens still refuse to acknowledge the fact of the terrible crimes committed by the Japanese military more than half a century ago, in Korea and in China, before and during World War II, nor have they shown any willingness to ask forgiveness. In addition to brutal concentration camps and large massacres of unarmed populations, these crimes include using human beings as guinea pigs for medical experiments and forcibly enlisting tens of thousands of Korean women to serve as prostitutes for Japanese soldiers.

True, the world media have reported some widespread speculation and soul-searching in Japan, following the recent crimes allegedly performed by the Aum Shinrikyo cult, whose members are described as talented intellectuals.[8] The leader and members of this cult are suspected of the gassing of a Tokyo subway in which twelve were killed and hundreds wounded, and of other crimes. Recently the leader of the cult confessed to the gassing. Japanese scholars have been quoted as saying that the appeal of such cults among many Japanese intellectuals results from the existential ache of many talented Japanese when faced with their vacuous life and society. Nevertheless, I have found no Japanese scholar who has dared to confront the entire neo-fascist corporate-capitalist political system, which breeds mediocrity and spiritual vacuity. Even if there were such a scholar (Wolferin also failed to find one), the capitalist-run media in Japan and other capitalist countries would probably not publish such a view. In short, the publicized soul-searching in Japanese society is merely a form of intellectual masturbation.

How could it be otherwise? Like Erik Krough, the leaders of Japanese society have almost never made decisions on the basis of adherence to moral or ethical principles, nor have they been called to task within Japan for their repeated immoral decisions. Instead, the society has prided itself on the fact that, through deceit, exploitation, and oppression, Japanese businessmen have created unprecedented wealth for a few, while contributing nothing spiritually worthy to the world we humans share together.

Consequently, again like Erik Krough, the elite that governs Japan lacks integrity. It is honored in the world for its wealth and its clever ways of making money—and for nothing much more. Like Aunt Augusta, Japan is a seductive success story.

∾

What about Monsignor Quixote? He is a comic figure, yet one intuits that he has attained integrity. Even though he tries to confront his bishop and struggles against the blasphemy of the "Mexicans," one can hardly call him an unsung hero. Why do Monsignor Quixote's rather foolish failures help him to attain integrity?

Integrity requires a willingness to remain innocent, in the Biblical sense of the word. In the Bible, innocence is attained when a person unites the wholeness of his or her being to relate personally to God or to other people. Indeed, a divided person cannot relate wholly or innocently. Note that this kind of innocence differs from the mad innocence of Pyle or of Rycker, which is condemned in Greene's novels, as discussed in previous chapters. Through the divided evil characters in his novels, Greene shows clearly that what Martin Buber described in his Biblical studies is very relevant. Genuine innocence is dialogical. Mad innocence is monological and often fanatic.[9]

The truth of the matter is a bit more complex. A person like Pyle, Rycker, Erik Krough, or Aunt Augusta, whose daily choices and responses block all possibility of dialogue, has also blocked all possibilities of relating wholly, innocently. These evil characters have entered a vicious circle, which, as Greene shows, is quite prevalent in capitalist society. In such a circle, a monological person embraces a mad innocence to justify his or her evil deeds, and this mad innocence ensures that he or she can never relate dialogically.

We need not wonder. Capitalism, as a system based on greed and survival, and the philosophy of Thomas Hobbes (which puts a price on every person), is anti-dialogical and anti-innocence. It demands that one always calculate or "reckon," as Hobbes called this attitude. But persistent calculating blocks dialogue.

To conceal its spiritual poverty, the supporters of capitalism present it in a very seductive way, as Aunt Augusta presents her life. Seemingly, this regime helps every person to pursue his or her own interests and to obtain many consumer goods. The truth is that capitalism, as a political and economic system, relates to all persons solely as pursuers of profits and as a means to profits. To succeed in capitalist society, one must know how to manipulate other people, cleverly and very often brutally, so as to obtain profit. Common language, which calls this relentless striving for success "a rat race," discloses its inhuman aspects. Indeed, like the evil characters in Greene's novels, the committed capitalist never relates to other people as ends in themselves.

Put differently, even though Immanuel Kant wrote his ethics for the bourgeoisie, his principles and his rational demands that we always relate to fellow human beings as ends are scorned by people who resemble Erik Krough. I am pointing to the leaders of transnational corporations and their many supporters who exploit and economically oppress hundreds of millions of people in the Third World, allowing many to live in abject poverty while the profits from their economic manipulations are fabulous. These capitalists never view other persons as worthy ends or as potential partners in dialogue in the world that we share and for which we are all responsible.

Hence, as the discussion of Japanese society has revealed, the capitalist regimes are quite comfortable with spiritual vacuity. Note also that the religious fanaticism of Rycker, who views all persons as means to obtaining an abstract religious principle, accords very well with his success as a capitalist. The resurgence of a fanatical and often violent Christian fundamentalism in the United States is just one example of the amiable cohabitation between capitalists and inane, wicked fanatics who resemble Rycker. In contrast, Monsignor Quixote relates wholly, innocently, to whomever he meets, including evildoers. This manner of relating is what helps him slowly to establish genuine friendship with Sancho and to obtain some wisdom.

All of Greene's unsung heroes are dialogical persons who retain some innocence. In quite a few instances, they strive to relate wholly, in dialogue, to other persons.

Here are a few examples. Ida relates dialogically to Rose. The whiskey priest relates dialogically to the lieutenant. Brown relates dialogically to Doctor Magiot, to Mr. and Mrs. Smith, and even to Jones. Fowler relates in dialogue to Pyle. D. and Rose Cullen relate dialogically to each other; in fact, D. strives to relate dialogically to whomever he encounters. Dr. Czinner attempts to relate dialogically to his fellow passengers on the train, as Maurice and Sarah Castle relate dialogically to each other in *The Human Factor* and Arthur Rowe strives to relate dialogically in *The Ministry of Fear*. Thus, relating dialogically ensures that Greene's unsung heroes retain their innocence. This innocence is a component of their integrity.

I concede that Monsignor Quixote's innocence is frequently quaint, childish, and even stupid. Often it borders on the naive; at times, it is indeed funny. Greene shows, however, that this childish innocence encourages moments of genuine dialogue between Monsignor Quixote and Sancho. They confront each other; they confront issues honestly, seeking truth. They courageously perceive many of the evils that they encounter, and Monsignor Quixote ackowledges that much of this evil stems from Franco's wicked fascist legacy and from the unswerving support given him by the Catholic Church. These moments of genuine dialogue lead to true friendship between Quixote and Sancho. And true friendship, as has been repeated countless times since the Bible described Jonathan and David or since the days of Socrates and Plato, often serves as a basis for soundness of moral character.

True, Monsignor Quixote is hardly an unsung hero. His failures are often the result of a childish stupidity. Yet, through his innocence and his limited struggle to adhere to moral and ethical principles, he does attain some integrity.

∾

Someone may say, Let me thrust a stick into your spokes. I want to consider Rycker from a novel perspective. At the end of *A Burnt-Out Case*, he confronts and kills Querry in a moment of innocent rage. Although his married life has failed, Rycker repeatedly proclaims that he adheres to moral and ethical principles. Why do you deny him integrity? Why do you deny integrity to the fanatic who announces that he or she adheres to religious moral principles? You know that those Palestinians who blew themselves up, in order to kill Israeli soldiers and to halt the peace process in the Middle East, gained much respect in some segments of their society.

The basic reason the fanatic does not attain integrity is that he or she lives in bad faith. Rycker's supposed innocence, like that of Alden Pyle, is false, at times mad. Furthermore, Rycker is so engrossed in proving to himself that reality accords, or should accord, with the Christian principles and beliefs that he fervently embraces that he is unable to relate dialogically to anyone. He never listens to his wife or to what Querry tells him. His ears are blocked against hearing anything that will not fit his scheme of reality. Such attitudes and deeds constitute and support his continual lying to himself.

The lieutenant in *The Power and the Glory* is on the verge of a fanaticism similar to that of Rycker. He also is willing to kill for his principles, yet, unlike Rycker and Pyle, the lieutenant senses that his attitude and decisions are corroding his being, his morality. Rycker and Pyle are both caught in the web of their own self-deceptions. They have abandoned all lucidity, all possibility of dialogue, and have decided not to perceive the evil that they do. The lieutenant is already enmeshed in the stickiness of bad faith, yet, again unlike Rycker and Pyle, he perceives that his world is out of joint. Because of his limited authenticity, the lieutenant may yet be redeemed.

Thus, Greene's characters show that a supposed adherence to moral and ethical principles that is done in bad faith is a dead end. Such an existential attitude of self-deception blocks genuine dialogue and the perception of truth. It may lead to daring acts, like Rycker's murdering Querry or Pyle's rescuing Fowler, but it is essentially a very cowardly way of life. Indeed, any person who refuses to perceive truth and persistently evades dialogue is a coward. Even if such individuals proclaim a deep adherence to a set of moral or religious principles, they will never attain integrity.

~

I have not yet mentioned that Greene's unsung heroes frequently obtain wisdom. It could hardly be otherwise, since wisdom is linked to simple courage and trust in the world, to innocence and to integrity, to seeing evil and to sensitivity to horror. In today's world, Greene's novels suggest, wisdom can begin to emerge when a person chooses to transcend the spiritual infantility promoted by corporate capitalism and the seductiveness of its consumer-oriented way of life. Wisdom, these novels repeatedly indicate, is also linked to fighting evil. Discussing the wisdom obtained by Greene's unsung heroes requires a new beginning.

NOTES

1. Alexander Herzen, *Childhood, Youth, and Exile*, trans. J. D. Duff (Oxford, England: Oxford University Press, 1980), 112–13.

2. See, for instance, Haim Gordon, *Dance, Dialogue, and Despair: Existentialist Philosophy and Education for Peace in Israel* (Tuscaloosa: University of Alabama Press, 1986); Haim Gordon, *Make Room for Dreams: Spiritual Challenges to Zionism* (Westport, CT: Greenwood Press, 1989); Haim Gordon, *Quicksand: Israel, the Intifada, and the Rise of Political Evil in Democracies* (East Lansing: Michigan State University Press, 1995).

3. A. A. DeVitis, "Religious Aspects in the Novels of Graham Greene," in Harold Bloom, ed., *Modern Critical Views: Graham Greene* (New York: Chelsea House, 1987), 86.

4. Immanuel Kant, *Groundwork of the Metaphysics of Morals*, trans. H. J.Patton (New York: Harper & Row, 1964), 106.

5. Two additional examples are Paul O'Prey, *A Reader's Guide to Graham Greene* (London: Thames and Hudson, 1988) and Neil McEwan, *Graham Greene* (London: Macmillan, 1988).

6. Søren Kierkegaard, *Fear and Trembling/ Repetition*, trans. Howard V. Hong and Edna H. Hong (Princeton: Princeton University Press, 1983).

7. Karel van Wolferin, *The Enigma of Japanese Power* (New York: Vintage, 1990), 209–10. This book describes in vivid detail the lack of spirituality in Japan.

8. See, for instance, *Newsweek*, May 29, 1995.

9. See, for instance, Martin Buber, *Kingship of God*, trans. Richard Scheimann (New York: Harper & Row, 1967); Martin Buber, *The Prophetic Faith*, trans. Carlyle Witton-Davies (New York: Harper, 1949).

Part III

THE WISDOM OF UNSUNG HEROES

9
Comedians and Tragedy

According to a Jewish legend, when Moses stood with the Children of Israel on the Egyptian shore of the turbulent Red Sea and the Egyptians' chariots were coming closer, God told Moses, "Raise your staff over the Red Sea and the waters will part."

Moses raised his staff. The tempestuous waters did not part. Moses froze, his hand uplifted, not knowing what to do. Nachshon Ben Aminadav approached, jumped into the raging waves, and the sea parted.

The lesson of the legend is clear. God's word and the staff of Moses, His dedicated *Navi* (prophet) and Israel's greatest leader, could not part the waters of the Red Sea without the jump of Nachshon Ben Aminadav. Note that Nachshon is a simple person, not a glorious hero. Still, the legend indicates, Nachshon's jump was necessary for God's word to become a reality.

Greene's unsung heroes often resemble Nachshon Ben Aminadav. They are not great leaders. No history books would describe the deeds of people similar to Ida Arnold or Thomas Fowler. Yet, in a pregnant moment, such people courageously jump into troubled waters, while others hold back and wait. Their jump frequently creates a new reality; their heroism seems to open an arduous path that others may follow. Along this arduous path, people fight an existing evil; frequently the path also leads to a life of freedom in which they live for things that are worthy.

By pursuing such a life, a person often attains wisdom. Even the legend points to such an outcome. Note that the Decalogue was given to the Children of Israel *after* Nachshon's jump into the waves, *after* they crossed the Red Sea and began to live the trials and tribulations of a life of freedom in the desert.

〜

Perhaps Greene's most vivid unsung hero who dares to jump into troubled waters, fight evil, and attain freedom, wisdom, and integrity is Doctor Magiot in *The Comedians*. Magiot is not a central character in the novel, yet his way of life is exemplary and inspiring when compared to most of the other characters. These characters often resemble unsuccessful comedians, who play their roles in an evolving farce of horror. Before turning to what can be learned from the lives of these sorry comedians, as well as the struggle some of them undertake to transcend this sordid role, consider Doctor Magiot.

He is no comedian. He plays no role and does not bluff in order to sell himself; nor does he play the fool in order to tell the truth. Doctor Magiot has transcended the need to play roles. He is perceptive, honest, authentic, and soft-spoken. He lucidly sees evil, both the evil of particular individuals and the evil of institutions and governments. He acts with simple courage and trust in the world. He is very much involved in struggling to bring some good to Haiti, that area of the world in which he has chosen to live. He is sensitive to the horrors of life in Haiti stemming from the abominable evils of Papa Doc Duvalier, who is supported by the government of the United States. He courageously supports those who fight these evils. His sound moral character and honesty are evident at first encounter. What is more, Magiot's worthy being-in-the-world leads to wisdom. Here are two examples of the wisdom attained by this non-comedian medical doctor.

How should a person struggle against the rampant evil of Papa Doc Duvalier and other wicked dictators who are firmly supported by the United States and its Western allies? Doctor Magiot is wary, and he does not suggest that people should die for their beliefs. He explains this view at a dinner hosted by Brown for himself and Mr. and Mrs. Smith.

Magiot's response does not satisfy Mrs. Smith who, donning the armor of democracy and interracial gallantry, refuses to see the many bizarre and brutal evils staring her in the face in Haiti. Likewise, she does not see that these evils stem from U.S. policies. She therefore chides Magiot for his timid approach. He answers: "In the western hemisphere, in Haiti and elsewhere, we live under the shadow of your great and prosperous country. Much courage and patience is needed to keep one's head. I admire the Cubans, but I wish I could believe in their heads—and in their final victory."[1] Is Magiot's answer timid? I think not. Consider just one of many recent historical examples.

Did Archbishop Romero keep his head when he wrote a letter to President Jimmy Carter asking him immediately to stop supplying arms to the government of El Salvador, which supported the death squads in its country? I do not know. Romero paid for that letter with his life, for he was soon gunned down by a member of the death squads that he forcefully condemned. Even today in El Salvador, despite the so-called peace accords, what the Western media termed "a free election process" was really a farce. Many lesser dignitaries than Archbishop Romero, such as union leaders, left-wing students, and others who had spoken out for the poor and the needy, paid with their lives during the election campaign. They were killed by soldiers and civilians who work for the fascist rulers supported and armed by the United States.

Look again at Doctor Magiot's question. In situations where wicked fiends rule unmolested, as in Indonesia, Guatemala, and El Salvador today, and in Haiti as described by Graham Greene, in regimes supported by a powerful, great, and prosperous country like the United States, is it wise or responsible to tell people to die for their beliefs? Magiot says clearly that it is both unwise and irresponsible. His sagacious statement is based on his experience in Haiti.

Magiot perceives that personal martyrdom against the brutal evils of the ruling regime in Haiti, which—let us not forget, even for a moment—is wholeheartedly supported by the United States and its capitalist elite, is totally ineffective. Only a concerted effort by many simple people in Haiti may alter the situation. Philipot and his small company may be the beginning of such a concerted effort. Furthermore, Magiot probably knows that martyrdom against the regimes supported by the United States and its allies, however wicked these regimes may be, is very often banished from the mainstream media in the United States and other Western countries because it may anger the regime or members of the corporate elite. Hence, it may even disappear from history.

Of course, courage and patience do not always suffice. But, as Magiot points out correctly, when fighting political evil in the Caribbean and Central America, one must keep one's head or be eliminated immediately by the evildoers. In such a desperate situation, where evil easily triumphs, what can sustain a person who fights against evil? Doctor Magiot's last letter to Brown contains additional wisdom.

～

In that letter, Magiot explains that there is a mystique to Marxism as there is to Catholicism. Ignoring this mystique, which Magiot does not explain, leads to foolish generalizations, like those of Mrs. Smith. Although the mystique is not conceptualized in *The Comedians* (and Magiot makes no attempt to explicate it), it is evident that a mystique informs the core of a faith in any authentic struggle against evil and for a just world. Put differently, the mystique is an essential component of a wish to establish a much better world, where evil will not thrive. Accepting this mystique, Magiot indicates, can lead to breaking out of the indifference—an escape that characterizes most people who are able to fight evil in contemporary established society.

As indicated previously, Magiot would probably endorse Chomsky's view that the widespread indifference that prevails in most contemporary societies is encouraged by a large majority of the capitalist leaders—most of them evil.[2] In addition to struggling against indifference, accepting the mystique of faith is also a way of living fully, not as a comedian. Comedians, who are persons who live a bluff, often thrive on the indifference of other people. Magiot hints that indifference is ruinous to one's entire being and to the world which we share.

These thoughts accord with those of Nietzsche's Zarathustra who encounters insipidity and indifference to his challenging message, as well as to the responsibility of being human, when he decides to bring his wisdom to a nearby city in the first pages of *Thus Spoke Zarathustra*.[3] Is not faith in the superman Zarathustra's mystique? Indifference is ruinous, Zarathustra suggests, because it is a sinking into an attitude of never-resolutely-questioning oneself or society. This attitude of never-resolutely-questioning is a flight from responsibility, creativity, thinking, the active pursuit of justice, and ultimately the glory that only humans can attain because they can do great deeds, utter worthy thoughts, think, and be creative.

It has already been indicated that, for Greene, genuine glory is quite different from the false glories that capitalist and other societies promote. *The Comedians* opens with Brown wondering if the false glory attained by Jones, the bluffer and petty swindler who has died in Haiti, differs substantially from that of the British generals and politicians whose statues adorn the streets of London. Were not many of these generals bizarre comedians, indifferent to the injustices in the world, and living a bluff, in much the same manner that Jones has lived his bluff?

How does a person daily reject this indifference, which is promoted by today's political leaders? Magiot's answer is through faith, though he does not specify which faith. It is evident to him that any non-fanatical faith that encourages a person to bring about less injustice in the world will suffice, although he does not spell out why faith is so important. Yet, if he were asked, "Why faith?" we can safely assume, on the basis of his way of life, what Magiot's answer would be. From his life and his letter to Brown, we learn that Magiot seeks partners who, together with him, will struggle to bring into being a world without the horrid injustices that currently prevail. He recognizes that, to embrace such a commitment honestly, the mystique of a faith in the possibility of a better world and in the dignity of one's fellow human beings is necessary.

Why faith? Because faith in the possibility of bringing about the Good and in the dignity of fellow human beings, Greene suggests, is itself a key to a better world and a worthy life. In human history, faith has helped to bring about much good, despite the perversions and distortions of faith that have often emerged. Furthermore, without faith, a person may easily sink into indifference or adopt cynical attitudes—or both. People thus ruin their possibilities of living a worthy life. For instance, the cynical or indifferent person will almost never be able to establish relationships of genuine love or deep friendship.

Doctor Magiot's wise emphasis on faith illuminates the insipidity of those characters in Greene's novels who have no faith in struggling for a better world. These persons flee from confronting instances of evil that they encounter, whether done by institutions or by individuals. The Assistant Commissioner in *It's a Battlefield* and Henry Pulling in *Travels with my Aunt* come to mind.

~

What sort of people does Graham Greene portray as comedians? In a telling passage in *The Comedians*, he suggests that, in our contemporary world, many people choose to sell themselves falsely; they bluff. If the bluff succeeds, they may obtain wealth, honor, power, and widespread acclaim. Advertising in a capitalist regime, for instance, is usually merely a manner of bluffing that is deemed honorable. Presenting a bluff convincingly is what the professional comedian does on stage. Hence, the relentless pursuit of success, which often requires bluffing convincingly and is central to capitalism, encourages some people to convince others persistently to believe their bluffs. They live as comedians.

Those bluffers and comedians who take their bluffing seriously usually do not strive to attain wisdom or truth, or to pursue justice, beauty, dialogue, or love.

Furthermore, many of these people no longer care that they are living a bluff; they justify their embracing of deceit as a way of life. Some of them demand that living as a comedian be done in style. In *The Comedians*, Martha Pineda's husband, the ambassador, who probably knows that Brown has made him a cuckold, points out that being a comedian is an honorable profession. He adds, "If only we could be good ones the world might gain at least a sense of style. We have failed—that's all. We are bad comedians, we aren't bad men."[4]

The ambassador is wrong. Living a bluff cannot lead to a worthy existence. Jones is not a bad comedian; he has developed style and knows how to make people laugh. Jones, however, is not a good man. He is unscrupulous, often immoral. The horrors in Haiti do not disturb him. It seems that he could hardly care less about the pursuit of justice, love, or wisdom. Jones joins Philipot's rebels in Haiti only because he fears exposing his bluff about his supposed past as a commando against the Japanese during World War II. Furthermore, he is a fugitive, sought by the Tontons Macoute in Haiti and the police in Britain and the United States, with no money and few options for flight. From Greene's description of Jones, we learn that very often the comedian who develops style in order to support a bluff leads a lonely, distorted, and often wicked life. When Jones finally tells Brown the truth about his total lack of military experience and about his inability to establish genuine loving relations with women, his profound loneliness and inane, fraudulent existence become evident. Need I add that Jones is merely a petty capitalist who has failed?

⁓

Doctor Magiot's authenticity, courage, and wisdom help to stress a central theme of *The Comedians* and of other novels by Greene: Today many people resemble ineffectual comedians within an evolving tragedy or a farce of horror. If these comedians do not become aware of their situation and do not attempt to transcend it, they seldom attain wisdom. Indeed, one of the few ways to attain wisdom today is to stop bluffing and to transcend the situation that requires such a bluff.

Why do so many people resemble comedians? One reason is that people are taught to go through the motions of relating to life, without living fully. The major concern of these ineffectual comedians is to act a part successfully, through which they hope to gain approbation and applause. Every day they devote much energy to playing the role that they have chosen. From this perspective, Magiot's emphasis on faith is wise. Through his life and deeds, he indicates that when there is faith in the possibility of bringing into being a better world, coupled with the courage to act for this better world, a person may often transcend his or her previous role. Like Brown or, even better, Philipot, a person may choose to go beyond being a bland comedian in an evolving tragedy or a farce of horror and decide to fight courageously for a better world.

A willingness to see the truth and the facts concerning injustice help individuals to transcend their roles. Consider two instances in which both Mr. and Mrs. Smith, who have come to Haiti to set up a vegetarian center, transcend their rather comic roles and act spontaneously, courageously. By such actions, they are suddenly no longer comic figures or comedians. The first instance occurs when they try to stop the Tontons Macoute interference in the funeral of Doctor Philipot. The second takes place when Mrs. Smith stops Captain Concasseur's team of Tontons Macoute who are brutally beating and interrogating Brown after the voodoo ceremony. In both instances, the Smiths see evil for what it is. Their courageous actions are part and parcel of their deep faith in the possibility of a better world, which they believe can be attained through democratic means, and primarily by establishing centers dedicated to teaching the virtues of vegetarianism and encouraging people to abstain from eating meat. Their brave responses in the two instances mentioned, where brutal evil is evident, help to enlighten Mr. and Mrs. Smith that so-called legitimate politics in Haiti are part of a farce of horror.

Many of Greene's unsung heroes are courageous persons who have faith in the possibility of a better world, yet they too often act as comedians. In much of *The Quiet American*, Thomas Fowler plays the role of an objective observer who refuses to get involved. He persistently tries to sell himself to others as merely an objective reporter. This ploy does not work. Fowler's lucid observations of the horrors of the French colonial war in Vietnam slowly begin to demand a decision. His seeing the truth and the specific instances of evil that he encounters require taking a stand.

At first, Fowler adopts a general political view in which he condemns the evil of regimes and institutions: If the Western powers will allow the peasants of Vietnam to pursue their own humble way of life, without trying to impose upon them by force the Western capitalist system and its values, the world would be much better. Today, with the benefit of hindsight, which reveals that French and, later, U.S. military forces brutally killed millions of Vietnamese civilians, it is difficult to reject Fowler's decision and his wisdom. In this sense, the novel is indeed prophetic. But even in the period of the French war in Vietnam, Fowler's faith in the human ability to strive for a world that would respect the freedom of simple people is worthy and underlies his first, general decision.

To live in good faith with a general decision, however, you must at times take a stand on specific matters that relate to individuals whom you encounter. Other-wise, you may lose your self-respect and your integrity. Fowler takes his stand based on his general decision, after witnessing the unwarranted deaths, torments, and misery resulting from Pyle's bizarre and wicked political meddling. This specific decision propels Fowler out of the role of a so-called objective observer of the horrors of the war in Vietnam. He is no longer a comedian. He has learned a very important bit of wisdom common to many of Greene's unsung heroes: To be committed to justice very often means to be alone!

~

Someone may say: You are making it much too simple. Are you confident that before becoming committed to justice, before helping to murder Pyle, Fowler is merely an ineffectual comedian? Is it not overly simplistic to suggest that Fowler endeavors merely to report the horror and the farce underlying the French colonial war in Vietnam objectively? Do not good and evil intentions intermingle in Fowler—intentions that include his response to Phuong's decision to live with Pyle—and finally force him to choose? These questions lead to a new perspective on what it means to be a comedian.

Disclosing the truth, as William Shakespeare has shown, is often best done by the clown or the fool, who will not be punished if the truth offends, especially if it offends those who hold power. Consequently, the comedian or the comic figure, who is aware of the power and ability of comic responses to enlighten a situation and who is sensitive to the horror of the situation confronting him or her, can frequently present worthy insights and objective truths from within a sordid situation. Note that the intentions of such a comedian or fool, whether good or evil, do not concern us. What enlightens are the fool's words and deeds.

In *King Lear*, the perspective of the fool is objective and rather wise. He sees the true situation of Lear without the trimmings added by accepted falsities and bad faith. He perceives Lear's dotardly myopia, his stubborn stupidity. Yet objectively seeing the truth and becoming involved in what is happening on the basis of this seeing is dangerous, even for the fool. In order to avert the dangers of the truth that he ventures to disclose, the fool ardently plays the role of the comic figure. This approach allows him to tell Lear that he, also, is a fool.

Fool. Dost thou know the difference, my boy, between a bitter fool and a
    sweet one?
Lear. No, lad; teach me.
Fool. That lord that counsell'd thee
    To give away thy land,
    Come place him here by me,—
    Do thou for him stand;
    The sweet and bitter fool
    Will presently appear
    The one in motely here,
    The other found out there.
Lear. Dost thou call me fool, boy?
Fool. All other titles thou hast given away; that thou wast born with. (1. 4.)

Thus, Shakespeare shows that it may be wise, if one wishes to tell the truth in an evolving tragedy or farce of horror, to assume the role of a comic figure. Like Shakespeare's fool, however, this comedian or comic figure should be aware of the role that he or she has assumed and of the importance of telling the truth.

Thomas Fowler is no fool. Yet, in almost all his interactions with Pyle, Fowler attempts to tell Pyle the truth without the trimmings of accepted falsities, without bad faith, but often with a wry and painful humor. Again and again, he struggles against Pyle's choice of myopia and stupidity. Speaking with an innocence similar to that of Monsignor Quixote, Fowler is willing to admit that in his personal life he himself has often been a fool. By such acts, he hopes to enlighten Pyle as to Pyle's own choice of living an ingrained foolishness, based on his unswerving loyalty to the institution that he represents. Fowler fails to influence Pyle, much as the fool in *King Lear* fails.

Yet what of Fowler's intentions? They do not matter. As the Bible already shows, every person's heart entertains sordid and wicked intentions. What does matter are a person's words and deeds, and the way of life chosen through daily decisions. Fowler's relentless attempts to achieve dialogue with Pyle are significant; his expressed anger at Pyle's evil is important. His supposed hidden intentions, like many of my and your intentions, are opaque, often vague, and insignificant.

Is Thomas Fowler a comedian? Yes, like the fool in *King Lear*, he, at times, exposes his own foolishness to show Pyle that he is a much greater fool. Yes, during the days that he tries to play the part of the objective reporter who is totally uncommitted. But also no, because he knows how to question himself authentically, as Doctor Magiot knows—a questioning that requires good faith and often brings wisdom in its wake. And no, because he transcends the role of the objective observer and helps the communists murder Pyle so as to stop his evil deeds. Like Nachshon Ben Aminadav, Fowler jumps into the churning waves of history.

~

Someone may still object: Your linking Greene's comedians to comic figures is unclear. Does that comic figure, Monsignor Quixote, who is not a comedian, attain any wisdom? You must admit that this priest's responses to the evil and mediocrity that he meets on his short travels in contemporary Spain are quite childish, often foolish, and naive. What is the difference between a comic figure and a comedian?

The difference between a comedian and Monsignor Quixote is that the priest does not sell himself falsely. He does not bluff. His stubbornly innocent and quite childish way of life in a corrupt world is what makes him a comic figure. Indeed, childlike innocence is the key.

I agree that Monsignor Quixote does not attain much wisdom. The wisdom he does attain, however, is mainly thanks to his childlike innocence. In this book, Greene presents both the comic and the tragic aspects of his major character's genuine, unscheming, trustful innocence, which often brings him harm. Nevertheless, it also brings worthy insights, such as when Monsignor Quixote discovers that Karl Marx's writings are based on acute historical perspicuity. Greene indicates that Monsignor Quixote's rather childish innocence allows him to see the world without many of the stereotypes, prejudices, and foolish myths to which his myopic, banal, wicked bishop and other evildoers cling. Such freedom from stereotypes, prejudices, and foolish myths is necessary for the pursuit of wisdom.

In short, a childlike, unscheming, trustful innocence is frequently necessary in order to pursue wisdom. In *Thus Spoke Zarathustra*, Nietzsche suggests that the child is the final metamorphosis in the development of a person toward a creative and worthy life. This metamorphosis appears after that of the camel, who has burdened himself with the difficulties of authentic existence, and that of the lion, who has bravely rejected traditional values and announced the possibility of willing new values:

> But tell me, my brothers, what can the child do that even the lion cannot? Why must the preying lion still become a child?
>
> The child is innocence and forgetfulness, a new beginning, a sport, a self propelling wheel, a first motion, a sacred Yes.[5]

Nietzsche was hardly the first thinker who emphasized innocence as central to a worthy and creative life. Indeed, the significance of innocence, at times even a childlike innocence, and its links to a right way of life repeatedly emerges in the lives and the sayings of Socrates, the Hebrew prophets, and many other original thinkers and wise men and women of antiquity. As an example of such innocence, consider Socrates' prayer at the end of Plato's dialogue *Phaedrus*:

Dear Pan and ye other Gods who inhabit here, grant that I become fair within, and that my external circumstances may be such as to further my inward health. May I esteem the wise man rich, and allow me no more wealth than a man of moderation can bear and manage.[6]

In this prayer, replace "Pan and ye other Gods who inhabit here" with God. The prayer immediately accords with the approach to life of Monsignor Quixote, at least after he commences his journey through Spain with the mayor, Sancho. It also accords with the approach to life of quite a few of Greene's unsung heroes. Dr. Czinner, D., Rose Cullen, Anne Crowder, and the whiskey priest in *The Power and the Glory* all come to mind. To see evil and fight it, these characters sense, one must attempt, through daily deeds, to become "fair within." Socrates would say that it is difficult to fight evil when a person's soul is tainted with wickedness, when a person is not "fair within." Furthermore, as he indicates to Phaedrus, such a person cannot attain wisdom.

Plato repeatedly indicates that Socrates, because of his innocent search for wisdom and the Good, was frequently considered inane and a comic figure. Polus and Callicles ridicule Socrates in Plato's *Gorgias*. Aristophanes presents Socrates with derisive humor in his comedy *The Clouds*. I wish to emphasize this point. Socrates was no comedian, and yet, Plato and Aristophanes show that Socrates' persistent pursuit of wisdom was considered by many of his fellow Athenians to be comical, ludicrous, and stupid. His innocent approach to life did not help him to escape ridicule nor did it spare him the death penalty.

Much the same is true of some of Greene's unsung heroes. Their innocent struggle for the Good is often considered inane. From the whiskey priest's responses, we can conclude that his arduous odyssey is probably viewed as ludicrous and quite stupid by some of his fellow priests in the Catholic Church. Dr. Czinner is considered a defiant rabble-rouser by his military judges, a newsworthy curiosity by the representatives of the media. Brown is disparaged and scorned when he seeks a job with an international corporation in the Dominican Republic. And Monsignor Quixote, who is not much of a hero, is branded insane by his bishop when he innocently describes his simple adventures and new, undogmatic thoughts.

As the example of Socrates' condemnation and death reveals, real-life situations frequently embody much more stupidity and much more of the evil of institutions than is disclosed in even the best fiction. Some of such comic situations can rarely be captured in fiction. As already related, ten years after its publication, *The Power and the Glory* was officially condemned by the Holy Office of the Catholic Church "because it was 'paradoxical' and 'dealt with extraordinary circumstances.' "[7]

Fortunately, the condemnation seems not to have influenced the reading choices of many prominent Catholics, as Graham Greene recalled:

> Years later, when I met Pope Paul VI, he mentioned that he had read the book [*The Power and the Glory*]. I told him that it had been condemned by the Holy Office.
> "Who condemned it?"
> "Cardinal Pissardo."
> He repeated the name with a wry smile and added, "Mr. Greene, some parts of your books are certain to offend some Catholics, but you should pay no attention."[8]

~

Graham Greene includes both comic figures and comedians in his novels. They allow him to present the complexity of contemporary society from alternating perspectives. Often these perspectives blend, yet we can point to different emphases. The comedian indicates how bluffing has become a way of life for an entire elite that embraces capitalism, whose members crave both success and to satisfy their greed and other bizarre lusts constantly. Comic figures show how this elite refuses to see the truth about its inane, insipid, and very often evil existence.

Greene's novels and twentieth-century history also show that, in despising and condemning wisdom, contemporary societies do not differ significantly from the Athens of Socrates. Indeed, contemporary societies are often ruled by insipid comedians, who persistently live a bluff and are supported by a coterie of associate-bluffers. Ronald Reagan is merely an extreme example of such a destructive trend. These evil and hollow bluffers, as well as their aides, frequently consider a person who chooses innocently to pursue the Good (or to write about such a pursuit) as foolish or dangerous.

Unlike some of the wicked comedians that he describes, Greene's innocent comic figures are repelled by evil. They have not been desensitized by the barrage of indoctrination spread by the media that placidly accepts contemporary horrors. Like Socrates, they learn that contemporary wicked societies will frequently attempt to spit out any person whose innocent way of life and courageous decisions challenge the prejudices, stereotypes, accepted myths, and inanities embraced and propounded by those societies' evil regime. In its milder moments, an evil regime will brand these strugglers for Good comic figures.

Let me again answer the question about Monsignor Quixote. Unlike the comedians in Greene's novels, Monsignor Quixote does not bluff. His odyssey is comic because, in a world where greed and lust for power often reign unchallenged, where a search for truth is ridiculed and rejected, where cleverness takes precedence over wisdom, his innocent attempts to seek out the truth and to do Good seem foolish and out of place. Consequently, when he firmly takes a stand for the Good, Monsignor Quixote seems to be galloping with his lance straight into revolving windmills.

∼

In Greene's *Our Man in Havana*, the comic emerges because the world is run by comedians who take themselves seriously. In this novel, almost everyone is involved in bluffing everyone else. The blatant stupidity of always living a bluff is presented as comical.

Agents in the Secret Service are always selling themselves falsely to most people. They are always bluffing their friends, contacts, and much of the world. When Wormold begins bluffing the Secret Service, which is always bluffing much of the world, the stupidity and hollowness of the policy and of the officers of such an organization are exposed to all and sundry. Greene also shows that this ludicrous stupidity and hollowness are a result of the Secret Service agents always taking themselves seriously. In fact, they take themselves so seriously that they do not perceive that a person who lives as a bluff and always supports bluffs—as they do—loses his or her integrity and sensitivity to other persons. Hawthorne is totally insensitive to Wormold's worries when he notifies Wormold that foreign agents want to poison him. Greene also indicates that when one is constantly bluffing, it is almost impossible to obtain wisdom.

Greene's other novels about the Secret Service show a similar lack of wisdom among all its officers. In *The Human Factor*, Daintry senses, much too late, that covering up the evil doings and the bizarre bluffs of Dr. Percival will result in the loss of his own integrity and his sensitivity to other persons. He has firmly believed that one can live with integrity within an institution if one acts according to the basic, just rules of democracy. He does not comprehend that many, if not most, institutions will always bend the rules so as to justify the evil they do and their own existence. Accepting this bending of rules means joining the evildoers. When Daintry realizes what is happening to himself, it prompts him to send in his resignation.

In contrast, Wilson in *The Heart of the Matter* does not sense that his constantly living a bluff has led him to lose his integrity and sensitivity to other persons. Consequently, Greene shows, Wilson is hardly a person who can establish friendships or relate lovingly. Hollowness haunts his every word. Louise Scobie also lives a bluff—that of the dedicated, religious wife. Her choice of a passive egocentrism, which frequently resembles the egotism of a spoiled child, is paramount throughout the novel. Louise persistently steeps herself in bad faith and embraces self-deceit; hence, she is unable to relate lucidly to Wilson's passionate, yet hollow, declarations of love.

Unlike Wilson or Dr. Percival, comedians such as Philipot, Brown, and Martha in *The Comedians* do not ruin their integrity and their sensitivity to other persons. They are aware that their living a bluff is wrong, though they may decide to continue in their role for a time. As Greene repeatedly shows, in certain circumstances, such awareness may lead a brave person to stop living as a comedian and to perform courageous deeds that lead to a worthy existence. It may also lead to a limited wisdom.

But only if a person has the courage that the awareness of his or her being a comedian demands. Such rarely happens. Greene repeatedly shows that capitalist life firmly encourages people to flee this awareness, to be cowards, to support institutions even when they do evil. In *England Made Me*, Erik Krough, that clever representative of corporate capitalism, totally lacks the limited wisdom attained by Greene's unsung heroes. He constantly evades the awareness that he is living a bluff and that such a life is ruinous to his integrity, to his sensitivity to other persons, and to his soul. His flight is supported by the admiration and respect showered upon him by Swedish society, as well as by his great wealth.

Despite the portrayal of depressing and banal characters like Erik Krough, who are very common today and are supported by much of the institutionalized evil that prevails, Greene's novels are often encouraging. Repeatedly, the novels show that you need not live as a comedian, you need not live as a bluffer. You can transcend this situation of deceit into which contemporary life throws you, and jump into the tumultuous waves of history to attempt to bring a change for the better. Such a jump often brings in its wake wise insights.

NOTES

1. Graham Greene, *The Comedians* (London: Penguin, 1967), 177.

2. Noam Chomsky, *Deterring Democracy* (London: Verso, 1991); Noam Chomsky, *Year 501: The Conquest Continues* (Boston: South End Press, 1993); Noam Chomsky, *World Orders, Old and New* (London: Pluto Press, 1994).

3. Friedrich Nietzsche, *Thus Spoke Zarathustra*, trans. R. J. Hollingdale (Middlesex, England: Penguin, 1961). See especially "Zarathustra's Prologue," 39–53.

4. Greene, *The Comedians*, 134.

5. Nietzsche, *Thus Spoke Zarathustra*, 55.

6. Plato, *Phaedrus & Letters VII and VIII*, trans. Walter Hamilton (Middlesex, England: Penguin, 1973), 103.

7. Graham Greene, *Ways of Escape* (London: Penguin, 1981), 67.

8. Ibid.

10
Existential Wisdom:
Joy, Courage, Questioning

A nna-Luise, daughter of the wicked Dr. Fischer in *Dr. Fischer of Geneva or The Bomb Party*, lucidly sees her father's evil and detests it. She perceives that Dr. Fischer is satisfied with himself and with the wicked games that he plays with his wealth. She doubts that he has a soul. In moments of genuine dialogue with her beloved husband, Alfred Jones, she shares her revulsion and horror at her father's wickedness and at his inability to relate lovingly to other people.

Alfred Jones passionately loves Anna-Luise; he delights in and admires her spontaneity, balanced courage, and perspicuity. Anna-Luise's joy in giving herself fully in love to him, a cripple who has lost his arm in the London Blitz, at first astounds Jones. Greene indicates that such astonishment is quite normal. Simple, spontaneous joy, balanced courage, and a giving of oneself fully in love, as lived by Anna-Luise Fischer, are very rare. Are these wonderful attitudes linked to seeing evil and detesting it? I believe they are. They are also linked to wisdom.

Even before Socrates, and up to Martin Buber and José Ortega y Gasset, philosophers have stressed that the pursuit of wisdom is a mode of existence, a way of life. Many agree that among the characteristics of this life are a seeing and detesting of evil, as well as a simple, spontaneous joy, a balanced courage, and a continual questioning of the reality that one encounters. Thinkers have repeatedly indicated that a person who, in daily life, courageously sees and fights evil, will often express a simple, spontaneous joy —because he or she is doing the Good. The questions that such a person poses to reality while fighting evil may lead to wisdom. Alfred Jones is indeed impressed by the precocious wisdom of twenty-year-old Anna-Luise.

What is a balanced courage? In *Theaetetus*, Plato suggests that a balanced courage appears when a courageous person apprehends quickly but pursues knowledge with gentleness. Theodorus describes the courageous Theaetetus thus:

he has a quickness of apprehension which is almost unrivalled, and he is exceedingly gentle, and also the most courageous of men; there is a union of qualities in him such as I have never seen in any other, and should scarcely have thought possible; for those who, like him, have quick and ready and retentive wits, have generally also quick tempers; they are like ships without ballast and go darting about and are mad rather than courageous; and the steadier sort, when they have to face study, prove stupid and cannot remember. Whereas he moves surely and smoothly and succesfully in the path of knowledge and enquiry; and he is full of gentleness, flowing on silently like a river of oil; at his age it is wonderful.[1]

From what we know of Anna-Luise, she apprehends a situation quickly, correctly, and rationally; she is exceedingly gentle and most courageous. Hers is a balanced courage. Despite her lucidly seeing and profoundly hating her evil father, she does not go darting about like a ship without ballast. She establishes a life of her own, which she firmly distances and divorces from Dr. Fischer's life and his blatant wickedness. Her decisions and way of life are frequently wise. For instance, she sees clearly that Alfred Jones is not a person who would compromise with evil. Greene intimates that Anna-Luise's lucidly seeing Dr. Fischer's evil and her horror at that evil help her to grasp intuitively what is worthy.

Are the acts and decisions of Graham Greene's unsung heroes similar to those of Anna-Luise Fischer? Quite often they are. Do these heroes express in their lives an existential wisdom? Very often they do. Let us again briefly comprehend the lives of some of these heroes, this time from the perspective of existential wisdom.

Look again at Ida Arnold in *Brighton Rock*. Like Anna-Luise Fischer, Ida frequently apprehends a situation quickly and correctly. She sees evil and is willing to fight it; she boldly and persistently questions the accepted version of Hale's death, trusting her perceptions, yet she is also gentle and courageous. She lives a balanced courage, never darting around like a ship without ballast. She decides to find Charles Hale's murderers and goes about it patiently, surely, smoothly, and usually with gentle resoluteness. Ida bravely and rationally seeks every shred of evidence that might promote her quest. In contrast, Pinkie Brown is quick-tempered and daring. His wicked decisions and deeds, such as his evil manipulations of Rose and of members of his gang, often lack equanimity and level-headedness. Borrowing a phrase from Plato, Pinkie is "mad rather than courageous."

As Anna-Luise lucidly perceives her father's vile deeds, Ida quickly perceives Pinkie's evil manipulations and mad decisions. She concludes quite quickly that Pinkie is the enemy; in all probability, he has killed Charles Hale. At the end of the novel, she foresees his wanting to harm and perhaps kill Rose and swiftly moves to avert it. Ida grasps that there is no way of reaching dialogue with Pinkie; he is a monological person who never questions his perceptions of reality, never relates trustfully to others. It is evident to her that such a monological person flees the possibility of questioning the world and one's own direction. Ida perceives that Pinkie's only concern is holding on to his power and manipulating other people to this end. His daily decisions block all openness to dialogue. (Much the same is true of Dr. Fischer.)

Ida is also clever. After concluding that Pinkie has murdered Hale, she understands that she must now thwart the evil deeds he plans to do to cover up the murder. While continuing to seek the facts about Hale's death, she courageously struggles to save Rose from Pinkie's clutches. She is willing to lie and deceive in order to stop Pinkie's murderous rampage and to save Rose's life.

Ida is no busybody, as Pinkie, Rose, and some of Greene's shallow and insipid critics indicate, but rather a person with existential wisdom. Again and again, Ida explains that what guides her perceptions, decisions, and actions is her knowing right from wrong, and her wish to stop those who do wrong by doing what is right and convincing other people to do what is right. As I have elaborated at length in previous chapters, that knowledge and those deeds are based on her questioning of reality, her lucidly seeing evil, and her willingness to struggle against it.

Ida's life is joyful, both physically and spiritually. Her body, with its large breasts, exudes gaity. Her balanced courage blends with her good faith and helps to sustain her joy. She relates innocently, straightforwardly, and wholly to whoever is willing to listen and to partake even partially in dialogue. As already indicated, Ida is manipulative when struggling to thwart Pinkie's evil intentions and wicked deeds. But she is manipulative primarily when fighting evil. Let me say it again. Unlike Pinkie, Ida is a dialogical person. She knows that manipulating others is primarily a means to fight evil; it is not her way of life.

What constitutes Ida's existential wisdom? She is wise because she intuitively knows that courageously struggling for what is right is a way of life that is worthy; it can bring those involved in such a struggle much joy. This wisdom is simple, but few people embrace it or live it, either in Greene's novels or, unfortunately, in today's world. Ida repeatedly attempts to share this wisdom with others, but they shy away. They sense that such wisdom frequently requires questioning accepted versions of morality and reality. It often requires challenging strong institutions, such as the police. Many people—indeed, probably most—lack the courage that such questioning demands.

Ida is also wise because she intuitively relates dialogically, wholly, to people whom she meets; she knows that such a way of relating is worthy. Her dialogical manner of relating helps Ida to perceive clearly that evil people, like Pinkie, are monological persons, who will never respond dialogically. Furthermore, they will not pose questions that require rational thinking or that lead to assuming genuine responsibility for other people. Ida seems to perceive, though she does not articulate, that monological persons are divided in their being by their constant attempts to manipulate other people; hence they cannot engage in genuine dialogue or genuine sharing.

∼

Another unsung hero with existential wisdom is Rose Cullen in *The Confidential Agent*. In a previous chapter, I mentioned her attraction to D.'s beaten, bloodied face; she immediately perceives that D. is "medium honest"—about everything. Rose's spontaneous attraction to an honest person blends with her refusal to embrace the greedy cynicism, blatant mendacity, lust for wealth and power, and continuous support of evil that prevails in the capitalist milieu of London to which she belongs. She despises the dishonesty, the mistrust, the inanity, and the mediocrity that this lust and cynicism breed, and she is disgusted with its often blind support of evil. In her spontaneous, friendly response to D., Rose very much resembles Anna-Luise Fischer's immediate attraction to Alfred Jones.

Much of what I have said about Ida and Anna-Luise also fits Rose Cullen. She apprehends a situation quickly and correctly. She authentically and straightforwardly questions her encompassing milieu and the persons she meets. She questions D. and demands rational, genuine answers. His answers help her to conclude that she is right. D. lives honestly, authentically, generously. He is worthy of trust, support, and love. What is more, Rose lucidly perceives that he also despises the avarice and rampant lust for wealth and power of the capitalist elite. After befriending and falling in love with D., Rose is willing to join him in fighting some of the manifestations of this evil. Greene shows that by deciding to link her life with D.'s and by loving him come what may, Rose slowly becomes gentle and courageous. She no longer darts around like a ship without ballast, as in the first pages of the novel. Her balanced courage and quiet joy in sharing her life with a person whom she loves, who fights evil and struggles for things that are worthy, are most evident on the final page.

What constitutes Rose's existential wisdom? Consider one last time her simple decision to befriend D. after the shock of seeing his bruised, bloodied face. The novel suggests that something like the following goes through her mind: "D.'s honesty is extremely rare and worthy. He is a person whom I must befriend! Immediately!" Why is such a decision, which is courageous and uncommon, also wise?

Rose knows that she is choosing the Good. Even if this choice requires following an arduous path, it does not bother her. Thanks to her questioning, Rose has learned that all other paths before her are steeped in mendacity, deceit, greed, and lust for wealth and power. They cannot lead to the Good. For centuries, great thinkers have taught that choosing the Good requires the courage to choose the path of honesty and, along that path, to pursue things that are worthy. They have agreed that such a choice is wise. It is the only way to a deeper knowledge and to dignified deeds.

Furthermore, Rose comprehends D.'s personal excellence and his commitment to things that are worthy. This leads her to want to share her life with him, which includes helping him in his fight against specific evildoers. Put succinctly, Rose chooses to partake of the Good and to appreciate and seek excellence, which are wise decisions. She perceives that these decisions entail undertaking difficult challenges. Indeed, by her choices, Rose decides to live pretty much in accordance with the last sentence of Baruch Spinoza's The Ethics: "But all things excellent are as difficult as they are rare."[2]

Let me say it again. Rose's active struggle to share D.'s excellence and to partake in his formidable fight against evil is a first step toward wisdom. Did not Plato actively struggle to share Socrates' excellence and his difficult fight against evil?[3]

~

Rose Cullen, Ida Arnold, and Anna-Luise Fischer all perceive what is worthy. They actively pursue it. Unfortunately, very few persons choose to live such a wise mode of existence. To judge by Greene's novels and my personal experiences as an educator and a person who has struggled against evil, most people fear to pursue what is worthy even if they perceive it as the Good. Indeed, many, if not most, people are cowards. Borrowing a phrase from Kierkegaard, they dread the Good. This dread, this anxiety when faced with the Good, often leads to a renewed embracing of cowardice, to bad faith, and to wallowing in stupidity—while allowing evil to flourish.

Kierkegaard noted that not responding courageously to anxiety when faced with the Good can often lead to terrible personal results. In some instances, persons who flee this anxiety choose to be bewitched by evil. In *Macbeth* and other plays, Shakespeare portrayed such outcomes of anxiety when facing the Good. Macbeth and his wife are persons who respond to anxiety, when facing the Good, by choosing to be bewitched by evil. By this choice, doing evil becomes their engagement, their personal commitment, their way of life. In *Macbeth*, the horrors of such a life are clearly expressed by the Bard. Greene was aware of the wisdom enunciated in Kierkegaard's writings. In *Brighton Rock*, Rose chooses to be bewitched by Pinkie. The Good that Ida presents arouses her anxiety; she flees this anxiety into a firmer loyalty to Pinkie, to his evil deeds, and to his banal and distorted existence.

In *The Confidential Agent*, only Else and Rose Cullen perceive D.'s honesty and integrity, and they decide to help him. Unlike Macbeth and his wife, both Else and Rose Cullen have little anxiety when encountering the Good that emanates from D.'s being. They both decide correctly and wisely that an encounter with a good person may enhance their own being and often bring joy. The fact that Else is murdered because she befriends D. does not diminish the joy that she experiences in this brief friendship.

~

Hold it, someone may say. Does that solitary fleeing fugitive, the whiskey priest in *The Power and the Glory*, attain existential wisdom? Greene shows that the priest perceives very little of the evil of the Catholic Church—evil to which the lieutenant responds with profound hatred. In addition, he participates in only a few moments of genuine dialogue. Although the whiskey priest is courageous and often questions himself, his deeds, and the reality that he encounters, and although it is evident that during his difficult wandering and flights he attempts to do Good, one cannot call him a joyous person. Quite frequently, the whiskey priest sinks into obsessive thoughts about his own sins. Furthermore, his final major decision, to follow the half-caste to hear a criminal's deathbed confession and, consequently, to be caught by the authorities—a decision that will result in his own death—can hardly be called wise. In short, does Greene suggest that an unsung hero definitely obtains existential wisdom? And, what do you mean by existential wisdom anyway?

Yes, the unsung heroes in Graham Greene's novels definitely obtain existential wisdom. They obtain it because they, and especially their deeds, question the encompassing reality, the institutions that do evil, and some of the terrible instances of evil that prevail. Quite frequently, however, these heroes obtain wisdom in a roundabout manner, as a corollary of their decision to fight evil.

What is existential wisdom? Since Plato, the pursuit of wisdom has been considered to be the pursuit of a life guided by things that are universally worthy. To obtain existential wisdom, one must attempt to realize, through concrete actions in everyday life, the claims emanating from things that are considered universally worthy, such as justice, friendship, knowledge, truth, beauty, and love. Socrates, as portrayed by Plato, frequently attempted to obtain such wisdom through dialogues with wise people who visited Athens and ordinary people in the agora, through learning and rational questioning. The wisdom attained by Greene's unsung heroes is often a result of their struggling to realize the claims of justice in a society indifferent to these claims. Their wisdom is not only an appreciation and understanding of the difficulties of such a task; it is also a result of their learning, in their own lives, that such a struggle will often bring both anguish and spiritual enhancement.

A person may lead a secluded solitary existence during which he or she grinds lenses. Even if such a person writes works of wisdom and corresponds with noted European thinkers, as Baruch Spinoza did, it is not evident that he or she knows how to fight evil in the concrete circumstances in which it is encountered. We do not know very much about Spinoza's life; it would be hard to conclude whether he fought evil and realized the claims of justice in his everyday life. We do know that some famous philosophers did not know how to fight evil concretely. For instance, Martin Heidegger joined the Nazi Party in 1933 for a year. After he resigned from the party, Heidegger never related with wisdom to the evil of his own past, nor did he forcefully condemn the horrors of the Nazi Holocaust. He never acknowledged his terrible mistake. Indeed, in certain areas of his life, Heidegger seems to have had little existential wisdom.[4]

In contrast, consider the whiskey priest. He is totally immersed in the everyday world. True, he is hardly a joyful person. Yet his daily defiance of religious persecution often arouses a brave hopefulness and, at times, a bold cheerfulness among the peasants he meets and to whom he ministers. When such things occur, the whiskey priest has fulfilled his task and his personal commitment. His difficult experiences, his persistent struggling to perform religious services for those who have faith—despite the evil decrees of the regime—do result in his obtaining elements of wisdom. He repeatedly learns that his courage and struggle to do what is worthy, in the oppressive situation in which he finds himself, speak to the spirit of many simple Mexicans whom he encounters, among them those incarcerated by the regime. These people who are faithful to the spirit of his message will not betray him. They will silently choose to suffer the harsh circumstances imposed by the regime and not sell him for a monetary reward.

Let us again pose the question. What wisdom does the whiskey priest obtain? The whiskey priest encounters and learns to admire a genuine quest for spirituality, especially among the peasants and the simple people to whom he ministers. He vaguely perceives that this quest for spirituality is much worthier than the sanguine, counterfeit spirituality prevailing in many religious institutions and in the homes of many of the wealthy, satisfied people who lead and support the Catholic religious establishment. He comprehends—and this constitutes wisdom—that his simple acts of defiance often educate much better than any learned sermons that he might have presented. His decision to defy evil, to fight it by continuing to minister to the believers, opens up new vistas, new opportunities, new ways of comprehending the world, new experiences for himself and for some of those he encounters. These new experiences are essential for any pursuit of wisdom.

～

Thomas Fowler's existential wisdom is not joyous; it is primarily a result of his persistent, courageous, authentic, and rational questioning of the situations in which he finds himself. He passionately seeks knowledge and the truth. As part of this search, Fowler also often questions himself, his deeds, his society, and his assumptions about human existence. Unlike Alden Pyle or even Phuong, getting to the truth of a matter is central to Fowler's existence, even when it requires taking risks. For Fowler, the pursuit of truth is a personal calling; questioning is a way of life.

Someone may suggest that Fowler's resolute questioning accords with his vocation as a journalist. True. Nevertheless, it is also true that very few journalists are authentic questioners. In Chapter 7, I discussed the evil and the inauthentic questioning of the journalist Parkinson, in A Burnt-Out Case. Quite often, as Greene has shown in other novels, journalists merely report the scoops, the so-called news that their publishers and editors wish to convey to the public, or the facts that their government wants reported. In short, Greene is correct in portraying Fowler's pursuit of truth as exceptional, since quite a few journalists eschew the truth.

Because the support of evil enrages me, I wish to again give one of many examples, that shows that many so-called "top journalists" in today's major mainstream newspapers do not question the reality that they encounter. They do not pursue the truth. Noam Chomsky has shown in detail that, for decades, scores of journalists employed by the New York Times, the Washington Post, and other organs of the U.S. mainstream media reported on Central America and never questioned the mendacity of the U.S. government. They never questioned the fact that, in the name of democracy, the U.S. government repeatedly set up, supported, and today continues to support Central American dictators who oppress, kill, and exploit their indigenous people, as well as often using death squads to stay in power. The journalists of the mainstream press have almost never pointed out that these dictators aided and were buttressed by greedy multinational corporations with headquarters in the United States. In short, scores of mainstream journalists never seriously questioned the ongoing financial and military support by the United States of wicked Central American governments that brutally oppressed and harshly exploited the indigenous populations and that continue to do so today.[5] Indeed, as a journalist, Thomas Fowler is very exceptional.

Fowler's courageous and authentic questioning is a first step toward wisdom. Such questioning frequently leads to a comprehension of the truth, and it supports both Fowler's commitment to truth and his personal struggle to live in truth. It is highly dubious that such wisdom can be attained by the U.S. journalists, criticized by Chomsky, who consistently support evil by their deceitful reporting and their flight from questioning the reality they encounter in Central America. Moreover, as Jean-Paul Sartre has pointed out, questioning is a manner of countering the curse of bad faith that characterizes many human relationships. By countering bad faith, Sartre shows, questioning may help to unmask many of the evildoers who hide under a mask of bourgeois respect, communist adulation, or fundamentalist fanatical beliefs. Fowler's persistent and resolute questioning accords with Sartre's insights; it slowly unmasks the insensitivity toward human suffering and the support of political evil hidden under Alden Pyle's bourgeois respectability.[6]

In this context, it is important to emphasize a point made earlier. Fowler's resolute questioning in the cruel day-to-day war in Vietnam helps him not to lose his sensitivity to the deliberate, murderous oppression of the Vietnamese by the French soldiers, supported by other Western governments. He never becomes insensitive to the terrible human suffering that results from the political evil he repeatedly encounters. Again and again, Fowler lucidly sees the continuing military oppression and senseless killing of innocent Vietnamese people. It repeatedly arouses his horror. Retaining sensitivity and the ability to see evil, even in situations where evil thrives and cruelty is rampant, is necessary for a wise existence.

Greene also shows that modesty accompanies genuine questioning, because it is necessary for attaining some truths and wisdom. Fowler is modest, as is D. in *The Confidential Agent*. Both Fowler and D. know that courageous questioning allows a person to attain only glimpses of the truth. Full knowledge of the truth or of what is happening is never in one's pocket. Furthermore, the limited knowledge that one may have attained by questioning must constantly be sustained by entering into new experiences. In the Vietnam of the 1950s, as in the England of the 1930s that D. encountered, this renewal of knowledge may frequently require participating in dangerous undertakings.

Wait, someone may counter, where exactly do you perceive Fowler's wisdom? Especially since, as you have stressed, he attains only limited knowledge of himself or of truth in the complex reality of Vietnam that confronts him?

Perhaps the most profound aspect of Fowler's wisdom is that his questioning teaches him how little he knows. Indeed, Fowler's wisdom echoes that of Socrates: He is wiser than Pyle and many others in knowing very clearly how much he does not know.

$\sim$

To recapitulate: Greene's unsung heroes show how actively fighting evil may frequently help a person attain existential wisdom while living a worthy life. This theme is hardly new. It is already evident in the wisdom of antiquity, at least from Socrates to Cicero. What is new is that Greene has shown that such wisdom need not be confined to a specific elite. It is within the reach of simple people, like Anna-Luise Fischer, Ida Arnold, Rose Cullen, the whiskey priest, and Thomas Fowler; people like you and me.

NOTES

1. *The Dialogues of Plato.* Vol. 2, trans. B. Jowett (New York: Random House, 1937), 145.

2. Benedict Spinoza, *On the Improvement of the Understanding; The Ethics; Correspondence,* trans. R. H. M. Elwes (New York: Dover, 1955), 271.

3. See Plato's Seventh Letter in Plato, *Phaedrus & Letters VII and VIII,* trans. Walter Hamilton (Middlesex, England: Penguin, 1975).

4. Much has been written about Heidegger's involvement with Nazism. See, for instance, Victor Farías, *Heidegger and Nazism,* trans. Paul Burrell (Philadelphia: Temple University Press, 1989); Richard Wolin, *The Heidegger Controversy* (Cambridge, MA: MIT Press, 1993).

5. Noam Chomsky, *Necessary Illusions: Thought Control in Democratic Societies* (Boston: South End Press, 1989).

6. For more on this topic, see Haim Gordon and Rivca Gordon, "Sartre on Questioning Versus the Curse of Bad Faith: The Educational Challenge," in *Studies in Philosophy and Education* 15:3 (July 1996), 235–43. See also Haim Gordon and Rivca Gordon, *Sartre and Evil: Guidelines for a Struggle* (Westport, CT: Greenwood Press, 1995).

11
Political Wisdom: Power and Glory

Many thinkers have held that political wisdom means knowing how to use power to bring about justice, freedom, and other things that are worthy. A person who succeeds in using political power for these ends may be glorified. He or she may be admired, extolled, and revered. No such approval awaits those simple people who fight evil in Greene's novels. Indeed, the relation of Greene's unsung heroes to political wisdom is a bit more complex. They attain some political wisdom but without obtaining power and with very little glory.

By definition, no songs are written about unsung heroes, nor are such people lauded and applauded by large segments of the populace. They do not attain widespread reverence. The limited glory that they attain, as already mentioned, partially resembles the glory awarded to the Hebrew prophets. The citation from Martin Buber, quoted in Chapter 6, indicates that the Hebrew prophets spoke out for justice and true faith, yet they very often failed to achieve their missions. Their glory was in their struggle, in their relentlessly speaking and acting against prevailing evils. The only resource available to the Hebrew prophets in this struggle was their eloquence and the truth of their statements in relation to concrete events. There is one major exception: Moses, who did wield political power. For all the other prophets, if they did obtain power, it was limited to a concrete situation or to an event that engaged them, such as Elijah admonishing King Ahab for his murder of Nabot so as to confiscate his verdant flourishing vineyard.

Let me say it again. Greene's unsung heroes do not acquire power. A few may attain glory among some friends or acquaintances, but not much more. Many of these heroes fail in their ongoing struggle against evil, yet these heroes do obtain political wisdom. And the meager grandeur they attain is true glory, not mere celebrity.

An example worth repeating is Doctor Magiot in *The Comedians*, whose wisdom, including his political wisdom, was discussed in previous chapters. Like all of Graham Greene's unsung heroes, Magiot does not seek political power. He craves and struggles for justice. When confronted by the concrete evils and the terror instigated by Papa Doc Duvalier and his evil henchmen, Doctor Magiot is willing to risk his life to try to bring some semblance of justice to Haiti. He is killed by the Tontons Macoute, but, in the eyes of some of the other major characters in the novel, he attains true glory.

~

Hold it! someone may say. What is glory? How is it attained? How is it linked to the complex political wisdom that you suggest Greene's unsung heroes obtain?

The Random House Dictionary defines glory as "exalted praise, honor, or distinction bestowed by common consent." This definition is quite correct; the problem is that it does not distinguish between true and false glory. Yet such a distinction is necessary in any discussion of political wisdom. In ancient Greece and Rome, true or genuine glory appeared primarily in the political realm. According to Greek and Roman thinkers, glory was attained by people who struggle to do the right thing in the political realm, who try to bring about justice. In contrast, a tyrant who basks in his or her power could never attain true glory.

Greene's novels very much adhere to the classical distinction between true and false glory. True glory is bestowed by free people, who courageously judge right from wrong and bestow honor, distinction, or exalted praise upon a person for doing what is worthy. Such glory may often ensure that a person's worthy deeds become immortal. An example of true and immortal glory for a worthy deed is that of Moses for bringing the Decalogue from Mount Sinai to the Children of Israel.

In contrast, Plato pointed out, the tyrant by definition enslaves all the subjects in the polis; if glory is bestowed upon him or her, it is a false grandeur. False glory is obtained by seducing or forcing large numbers of people to consent to glorify an unworthy individual. In the twentieth century as in Plato's time, false glory is most evident in a tyranny or a dictatorial regime. Mao Tse-Tung, Ayatollah Ruhollah Khomeini, Alfredo Stroessner of Paraguay, and Idi Amin of Uganda were all dictatorial tyrants upon whom an enslaved and suffering population bestowed a false glory. In *The Comedians*, the glory bestowed upon Papa Doc Duvalier by his toadies and sycophants, as well as by officials from the United States, is false and quite obnoxious.

Greene shows, however, that false glory is also bestowed in democratic regimes. Think of the acclaim from which Querry in *A Burnt-Out Case* flees or the false glory bestowed upon Erik Krough in *England Made Me*. Today in many democracies, the bestowing of such false glory upon undeserving people who have never done a worthy deed is in full sway. Political figures who have definitely done terrible evils are often glorified. Just one example among many is the glory bestowed upon Richard Nixon at his death by scores of pundits writing in the mainstream media. These writers ignored the major evils and vile crimes of this mendacious and very wicked president. At times, it seems that in the reigning capitalist milieu, which, as Greene repeatedly shows, is usually governed by an elite of mediocrity, true glory has all but disappeared. Even the craving for true glory is frequently dissolved in the acidic bath of seductive inanity promoted by the media. Greene describes some of the powers of such seductive mediocrity through the acts and stories of Aunt Augusta in *Travels with my Aunt*.

Greene is not alone in distinguishing between true glory, such as obtained by Doctor Magiot who fights evil and craves justice, and false glory, such as that of Erik Krough who does evil. Listen to Martin Heidegger:

> To glorify, to attribute regard to, and disclose regard means in Greek: to place in the light and thus endow with permanence, being. For the Greeks glory was not something additional which one might or might not obtain; it was the highest mode of being. For moderns glory has long been nothing more than celebrity and as such a highly dubious affair; an acquisition tossed about and distributed by the newspapers and the radio—almost the opposite of being.[1]

The Hebrew language also seems to support Heidegger's statements. *Thilah*, which is the word for glory, seems to be linked to the word *Hilah*, which means light or halo of light. With these thoughts in mind, consider again the examples mentioned above. Through his worthy deeds, Doctor Magiot is placed in the light. His life and deeds attain a permanence worthy of regard in our mind. They can illuminate our way of life; they have being. His glory enlightens us. In contrast, the successful Erik Krough merely attains celebrity, and, as Greene shows, this celebrity is based on a shallow, insipid appreciation of Krough's wealth. It is indeed a highly dubious affair.

As mentioned, an important step toward wisdom in the political realm is learning to distinguish between false glory and true glory. This step may not seem difficult, but, as Greene shows, few people decide to take it for a rather simple reason. Here, once again, Greene's presentation accords with much that Heidegger wrote; distinguishing between true and false glory requires acting resolutely, authentically. It also requires thinking.

The lieutenant in *The Power and the Glory* succeeds in a major campaign by capturing and killing the whiskey priest. Yet he feels empty and unfulfilled; he faces anguish. This anguish, however, does not lead him to think or act differently. As the book ends, he still refuses to cast doubt on his ideas and beliefs. Fanatical devotion to a set of ideas is a decision not to think. It is a decision to flee from resolutely facing the anguish of living as a free person who can question reality, dogmas, or prevailing ideas. Need I add that when a person decides not to think, he or she will never comprehend the difference between false and true glory, between celebrity and the highest being?

Greene often shows that the decision not to think not only limits political wisdom but also leads to what Hannah Arendt has called the banality of evil: evil done by banal people. The bishop and his toady, Father Herrera, are examples of such banality and evil in *Monsignor Quixote*. The same is true of Parkinson and Rycker in *A Burnt-Out Case*. These characters have firmly decided not to think. The possibility of distinguishing between true and false glory never enters their minds. Small wonder that they have no political wisdom.

Political wisdom also means that, when faced with evil, one knows the limits of one's powers and knowledge. One learns these limits only by deciding to act. In the political realm, power is the ability to convince or force other people to do what one decides should be done. As Plato repeatedly emphasized, a wise politician will use his or her power to do worthy things, especially to pursue justice. When Greene's unsung heroes encounter evil they decide to act to fight evil people, despite their acknowledged lack of power and their limited knowledge. This decision leads them to obtain some important elements of political wisdom.

Consider, for instance, these questions: Can you break through a banal person's fanatical devotion to a set of ideas and thus stop him or her from doing evil? Can you convince wicked or greedy people—for instance, Erik Krough or Dr. Fischer—who have firmly chosen their vile way of life, not to do evil? The answer suggested by Greene's novels to both questions is an unqualified: NO! In many cases, this answer is correct.

Only by violence can a person stop Pinkie's or Papa Doc Duvalier's murderous rampage. Seemingly, Alden Pyle is a more complex case. Greene indicates, however, that one cannot break through the arrogant self-satisfaction of Alden Pyle. Even though he has had a very good education, he cannot be forced to think. The only ways to stop the evil of Alden Pyle are to change the orders he receives from his superiors, to have him recalled from Vietnam, or to kill him. Fowler recognizes that the latter possibility is the only one open to him. Indeed, Greene intimates that Fowler attains political wisdom by recognizing the limitations of his situation by deciding to have Pyle murdered, and by participating in the killing.

Someone may ask: Did Thomas Fowler obtain political wisdom, beyond his lucidly comprehending the evil deeds, inane excuses, personal ruses, and bad faith of Alden Pyle? Yes. Fowler learned from his anguish that a refusal to fight resolutely against the political evil instigated by Pyle would ruin his own soul, his humanity. Moreover, it seems that Fowler grasped that such a ruining of souls fits very well with the oppression and exploitation characteristic of the capitalist milieu, which he served and to which he belonged. The political wisdom that Fowler obtained can perhaps be summarized thus: Fighting the many political evils of Western capitalism is a way of fighting for your integrity, for the purity of your soul, and for the freedom, lives, and souls of many others. Fowler also learned, however, that such wisdom is meaningless if it is not translated into personal decisions and deeds, including deeds that will greatly harm evil people. You cannot retain your integrity and your soul if you refuse to fight evil!

Another unsung hero who learns a similar lesson is D. in The Confidential Agent. D. arrives in England as a confidential agent who merely wishes to conclude a coal deal for the fighters for freedom in his war-stricken country. He does not want to fight the people who strive to interfere with his mission; these are often people who have supported the fascists who battled to usurp the legitimate government of his country. He hopes to evade these enemies or perhaps to outsmart them. Soon D. recognizes that his powers are very limited. Like Fowler, however, at a certain moment, D. concludes that any additional compromise with the evil deeds constantly being done to him, to his supporters, and to the people he represents means betraying justice and losing his integrity as a human being. He decides to fight. This decision is wise.

~

Wisdom is also the knowledge that when one takes a stand against political evil, both grave dangers and unforeseen opportunities for bringing good may emerge. Even to comprehend such opportunities, according to Doctor Magiot in his last letter to Brown, genuine faith is crucial. Magiot therefore pleads with Brown not to abandon faith. As already argued, such faith often means relating innocently and trustfully to the world, without the insidious cleverness and blunt brutality that characterizes many evildoers. It also means scorning the celebrity that, with the help of the capitalist-oriented media, masquerades as glory. Note that Querry in *A Burnt-Out Case* might have been able to regain his faith if he had not been killed by Rycker; he took the first step when he fled from the mendacious celebrity engulfing him, a celebrity that he despised because it crowned him with undeserved false glory.

In *The Comedians*, Mr. and Mrs. Smith, despite their many failures, never abandon genuine faith—in their case, it is faith in the profound and broad human benefits arising from a vegetarian diet. Because it is genuine, their faith transcends the goals of spreading a specific teaching. With simple spontaneity, they relate courageously and generously to the people whom they encounter. Greene shows that, in today's harsh world, the Smiths' actions frequently seem ludicrous, naive, or both. People mock them or seek to take advantage of their supposed naïveté. He also shows, however, that Mr. and Mrs. Smith know how to dismiss mockery by relating dialogically. They are also prudent and wary. They carefully evaluate the attempts of corrupt politicians to cheat them, and, when they see no honest opening in Haiti, they pack up and leave. In short, they are willing to learn from their engagements and failures, while never giving up their struggle to bring good. Hence, they never succumb to the widespread cynicism so common in the political realm, which often erodes a person's soul. Greene seems to indicate that Mr. and Mrs. Smith's slow plodding attainment of political wisdom should be appreciated.

In contrast, Henry Pulling in *Travels with my Aunt* is closed to attaining any political wisdom. Steeped in tedious boredom in his everyday life, he is happy to be seduced by the stories and actions of his unscrupulous aunt/mother. Quite soon, Pulling willingly joins her, actively participating in her bizarre and evil undertakings. As already mentioned, Pulling is the epitome of capitalist mediocrity. This successful, retired bank manager has no genuine faith, no willingness to take a resolute stand against evil, no appreciation of true glory. And, of course, he never thinks.

Henry Pulling's inane decisions and his demeaning responses to his aunt's seductive evil accord with an important principle that appears in Book I of Plato's *The Laws*: Political wisdom begins with the resolve to withstand seductions. Plato suggests that learning to drink wine moderately may help a person learn how to withstand the seductiveness of vile pleasures. This discussion of seductions in the political realm precedes many of the ideas and thoughts presented in the succeeding books of *The Laws*. Plato believed that a person who does not learn to withstand the seductions of lowly pleasures will not struggle for justice. In addition, such a person will never attain political wisdom.

The seductiveness of evil people is hardly a problem for Greene's unsung heroes. Before the reader meets them, these heroes have learned to distinguish between right and wrong; they emerge in Greene's novels as persons who refuse to become desensitized to the sufferings that result from evil deeds, and they are willing to act against evil. They often scorn the evil people whom they encounter. Like Ida in *Brighton Rock* or the whiskey priest, they may attain only a limited wisdom, especially in the political realm. Still, they show us that by regarding the seductiveness of evil with disdain, one can project one's life onto a higher plane of existence. These unsung heroes have reached a level whereby their deeds transcend acting merely to obtain earthly pleasures or general acclaim. For anyone who adopts such an approach, obtaining political wisdom is a genuine possibility.

Martin Heidegger was right in holding that, in contemporary life, celebrity, which almost never has anything to do with worthy deeds, has eclipsed true glory. In the United States, mediocre clever people like Donald Trump or Ronald Reagan, who do evil and often support evil, bask in celebrity. Intimate sordid details of their banal and often bizarre lives help sell newspapers and television programs. When the unbridled veneration of celebrity reigns unchallenged, as is quite common in the United States and in all other Western democracies, stupidity has triumphed. Thinking has vanished, as has wisdom.

Greene's unsung heroes who fight evil do not attain celebrity. Yet these heroes do choose to fight evil, which is frequently the only way to live a genuine, authentic, and thoughtful life in our world. This is especially true because, in this capitalist-oriented world, true glory, knowledge, wisdom, and many other worthy things are constantly eclipsed by celebrity. Moreover, through their lives these unsung heroes reveal that the choice to fight evil, including very often political evil, is a major step on the path to wisdom. Hence, by telling the stories of simple people who fight evil, Greene has shown that rays of true glory can still emerge from behind the glittering mendacity spread by celebrity.

NOTE

1. Martin Heidegger, *An Introduction to Metaphysics*, trans. Ralph Manheim (New Haven: Yale University Press, 1959), 103.

12
Conclusion:
Learning to Fight Evil

Graham Greene's novels are great literature. As such, they are educational, for they teach us about life. This book repeatedly suggests that they have much to teach us about fighting evil here and now, about endeavoring to live a worthy life. In novels that span fifty years of twentieth-century history, Greene related stories of evil persons who destroy the freedom of others and of a few simple people who fight them. Through these stories, he showed us readers three simple truths: First, evil exists; second, it is possible to fight it; and third, you may attain wisdom and, at times, a very limited glory by undertaking such a struggle.

Presenting these three truths abstractly does not resemble telling a story through which the truths emerge. In a story the truths become vivid, alive, and difficult to ignore. You, the readers, must take a stand. What do you condemn in Pinkie's acts and way of life in *Brighton Rock*? Should the whiskey priest in *The Power and the Glory* risk his life to hear the final confession of a dying murderer? What is admirable about D. in *The Confidential Agent*? What is despicable about Dr. Fischer in *Dr. Fischer of Geneva or The Bomb Party*? Taking a stand in response to these questions requires thinking and, in no few cases, assuming responsibility for your life. It is difficult and inauthentic to condemn Scobie's bad faith and cowardice in *The Heart of the Matter* and, some moments or days later, to refuse to question my own life, my cowardly acts, my bad faith. In short, Greene's novels confirm a well-known truth. Thinking and assuming responsibility for the world, as guided by the reading of great literature, are keystones of any worthy education.

Learning to fight evil is extremely important. The major reason is that evil deeds destroy human freedom; hence, they should be halted, eradicated from the face of the earth. But, as Greene's novels show, many leaders and ordinary people in contemporary society do evil. Many of their compatriots have learned to live comfortably with evil, to support it, to cover it up, to ignore its existence, to rationalize it away. A Hobbesian state of war in which a rampant greed thrives prevails unchallenged. Today, the result is a society in which banal, greedy persons attain respect and in which institutions sustain evildoers and support the spread of evil deeds. Liberal capitalism is one of the banners of this wicked way of life. Thus, Greene's novels repeatedly show: Western capitalist societies consistently legitimize evil and leave very little space for fighting it.

Greene's novels suggest, however, that, despite the difficulties, it is possible to utilize the limited space existing in a capitalist state to fight evil. Through the lives of their unsung heroes, many of his novels show what attitudes to life we should assume and what personal decisions are necessary for us to take so as to embark upon such a struggle. These attitudes and decisions also educate us as readers.

There is also a spiritual, down-to-earth perspective to the stories of the unsung heroes that Greene describes. Hannah Arendt has pointed out that the only way great acts and good deeds remain in the memory of a community is for someone to tell their story. That is the role of the historian. From a historical perspective, the memory of good deeds performed by many simple people who have fought evil is fragile. Very often, the stories told about these deeds are rapidly erased from the memory of a community. One reason is that the overall point of view adopted by historians emphasizes major trends. By such an emphasis, historians very frequently condemn the fragile moments of good deeds by simple people to obscurity. Another reason, repeatedly mentioned in this book, is that these deeds often challenge those in power.

Enter the novelist, and especially Graham Greene. His novels remind us of the dignity and integrity of people similar to you and me, people similar to his unsung heroes, whose important stories may have been unrecorded, forgotten, overlooked, or ignored. His novels also indicate that these unsung heroes, who live among us, may have attained wisdom. Hence, we should seek these people out and learn from them—about fighting evil and about living a worthy life.

～

Quite a few of Greene's unsung heroes are loners: Thomas Fowler and the whiskey priest immediately come to mind. Others encourage people to join them, either straightforwardly, as Ida Arnold does, or through the worthiness of their being, as when Rose Cullen joins D. It is evident that teams of people who fight evil can have greater effect. Greene also indicates, albeit not always clearly, that working together against evil in this way can be spiritually enhancing. Indeed, the loneliness of Thomas Fowler and the whiskey priest weighs heavily upon them; they find no persons with whom to share their difficult choices. No one they know is able to listen to the limited wisdom that they have slowly attained through their ongoing struggles. They recognize that, without such sharing, they are stuck within their own thoughts and deeds. Due to their loneliness, they are quite unable to comprehend these thoughts and deeds through the general perspective that sharing may provide.

Put differently, since fighting evil in contemporary society is so difficult, Greene's novels suggest to his readers: Try to find partners, people who will share the struggle with you. Working together with others is one of the best ways to learn how to fight evil and to struggle against evildoers. While fighting evil together, you will also frequently learn to live better lives. Is not such a seeking for partners who will join him in fighting the evil in Haiti central to the life of Doctor Magiot?

~

The book of First Samuel in the Bible relates the story of the brave young shepherd, David, who volunteered to accept the challenge of the arrogant Philistine, Goliath. When King Saul heard of David's decision, he told his servants to dress the young shepherd, who was preparing to go out to battle the Philistine, in his own coat of mail. However the armor was too heavy for David; he could hardly walk in it. He discarded it and went out to face Goliath armed only with his slingshot.

Graham Greene's unsung heroes also go out to fight evil without armor. It seems that any coat of mail would weigh them down when they decide to face the challenges of powerful, arrogant, evil persons. Some of these evil persons are protected by systems and institutions, such as the CIA, whose armament is much stronger than that of the Biblical Goliath.

Unlike the triumphant David, Greene's unsung heroes often fail. When they do not fail, their few victories never become topics of ballads or songs. I still remember dancing the hora thirty years ago, to a new tune for the song first sung by the Israelite maidens after David's resounding victory three millenia ago. The words of the song were taken from First Samuel, chapter 18, verse 6: "Saul has slain his thousands. And David his ten thousands."

Today, we have no giant Goliaths. Yet, arrogant evil people and cynical Goliathic systems and institutions continue to do much evil, deliberately destroying human freedom all over the world. Graham Greene's novels show that it is possible, worthy, and wise to struggle against these evil persons, these Goliathic systems and institutions; it is right to fight their pernicious deeds. But, his novels suggest, your situation resembles that of the young, brave David. There is no coat of mail that you can don that will not weigh you down. You must be willing to face these evil people and institutions with passion, pluck, courage, and a deep faith in the worthiness of your cause.

Selected Bibliography

Allain, Marie-Françoise. *Conversations with Graham Greene*. London: Penguin, 1991.

Arendt, Hannah. *Between Past and Future: Eight Exercises in Political Thought*. Middlesex, England: Penguin, 1977.

———. *Eichmann in Jerusalem: A Report on the Banality of Evil*. Middlesex, England: Penguin, 1976.

———. *The Human Condition*. Chicago: University of Chicago Press, 1958.

Bloom, Harold, ed. *Modern Critical Views: Graham Greene*. New York: Chelsea House, 1987.

Buber, Martin. *Between Man and Man*. London: Fontana, 1961.

———. *On the Bible*. New York: Schocken, 1968.

Chetley, Andrew. *A Healthy Business? World Health and the Pharmaceutical Industry*. London: Zed Books, 1990.

Chomsky, Noam. *Deterring Democracy*. London: Verso, 1991.

———. *Necessary Illusions: Thought Control in Democratic Societies*. Boston: South End Press, 1989.

———. *World Orders, Old and New*. London: Pluto, 1994.

———. *Year 501: The Conquest Continues*. Boston: South End Press, 1993.

Conrad, Joseph. *Heart of Darkness & The Secret Sharer*. New York: Signet, 1980.

———. *Lord Jim*. Middlesex, England: Penguin, 1977.

———. *The Nigger of the Narcissus/ Typhoon and Other Stories*. Middlesex, England: Penguin, 1986.

Cuoto, Mario. *Graham Greene: On the Frontier*. New York: St. Martin's Press, 1988.

Donaghy, Henry J, ed. *Conversations with Graham Greene*. Jackson: University Press of Mississippi, 1992.

Dostoyevsky, Fyodor. *The Brothers Karamazov*. Trans. Richard Pevear and Larissa Volokhonsky. New York: Vintage, 1991.

———. *The Possessed*. Trans. Constance Garnett. New York: Fawcett, 1966.

Engels, Friedrich. *The Condition of the Working Class in England*. Middlesex, England: Penguin, 1987.

Erdinast-Vulcan, Daphna. *Graham Greene's Childless Fathers*. London: Macmillan, 1988.

Faulkner, William. *The Hamlet*. New York: Vintage, 1991.

———. *The Mansion*. New York: Vintage, 1955.

———. *The Town*. New York: Vintage, 1961.

Galeano, Eduardo. *Open Veins of Latin America: Five Centuries of the Pillage of a Continent*. New York: Monthly Review Press, 1973.

Gordon, Haim. *Dance, Dialogue, and Despair: Existentialist Philosophy and Education for Peace in Israel*. Tuscaloosa: University of Alabama Press, 1986.

———. *Make Room for Dreams: Spiritual Challenges to Zionism*. Westport, CT: Greenwood Press, 1989.

———. *Naguib Mahfouz's Egypt: Existential Themes in His Writings*. Westport, CT: Greenwood, 1990.

———. *Quicksand: Israel, the Intifada, and the Rise of Political Evil in Democracies*. East Lansing: Michigan State University Press, 1995.

Gordon, Haim, and Rivca Gordon. *Sartre and Evil: Guidelines for a Struggle*. Westport, CT: Greenwood Press, 1995.

Greene, Graham. *Brighton Rock*. London: Penguin, 1966.

———. *A Burnt-Out Case*. London: Penguin, 1963.

———. *The Captain and the Enemy*. Middlesex, England: Penguin, 1989.

———. *The Comedians*. London: Penguin, 1967.

———. *The Confidential Agent*. London: Penguin, 1971.

———. *Dr. Fischer of Geneva or The Bomb Party*. London: Penguin, 1980.

———. *The End of the Affair*. London: Penguin, 1975.

———. *England Made Me*. Middlesex, England: Penguin, 1943.

———. *Getting to Know the General*. Middlesex, England: Penguin, 1984.

———. *A Gun for Sale*. London: Penguin, 1973.

———. *The Heart of the Matter*. London: William Heinemann, 1948.

———. *The Honorary Consul*. New York: Simon and Schuster, 1973.

———. *The Human Factor*. London: Penguin, 1978.

———. *It's a Battlefield*. London: Penguin, 1962.

———. *Loser Takes All*. London: Penguin, 1971.

———. *The Ministry of Fear*. London: Penguin, 1973.

———. *Monsignor Quixote*. London: Penguin, 1983.

———. *Our Man in Havana*. London: Penguin, 1962.

———. *The Power and the Glory*. London: Penguin, 1962.

———. *The Quiet American*. Middlesex, England: Penguin, 1962.

———. *Stamboul Train*. London: Penguin, 1963.

———. *The Tenth Man*. London: Penguin, 1985.

———. *The Third Man & The Fallen Idol*. London: Penguin, 1971.

———. *Travels with my Aunt*. London: Penguin, 1971.

———. *Ways of Escape*. London: Penguin, 1981.

———. *Yours Etc.: Letters to the Press, 1945–1989*. London: Penguin, 1989.

Herzen, Alexander. *Childhood, Youth, and Exile*. Trans. J. D. Duff. Oxford, England: Oxford University Press, 1980.

Hobbes, Thomas. *Leviathan*. London: Everyman's Library, 1914.

Hurst, Philip. *Rainforest Politics: Ecological Destruction in South-East Asia*. London: Zed Books, 1990.

Kant, Immanuel. *Groundwork of the Metaphysics of Morals*. Trans. H. J. Patton. New York: Harper & Row, 1964.

Kelly, Richard. *Graham Greene*. New York: Fredrick Ungar, 1984.

Kwitny, Jonathan. *Endless Enemies: The Making of an Unfriendly World.* Middlesex, England: Penguin, 1986.

Loewenson, Rene. *Modern Plantation Agriculture: Corporate Wealth and Labor Squalor.* London: Zed Books, 1992.

McEwan, Neil. *Graham Greene.* London: Macmillan, 1988

Nietzsche, Friedrich. *Thus Spoke Zarathustra.* Trans. R. J. Hollingdale. Middlesex, England: Penguin, 1961.

Nizan, Paul. *Aden Arabie.* Trans. Joan Pinkham. New York: Columbia University Press, 1987.

O'Prey, Paul. *A Reader's Guide to Graham Greene.* London: Thames and Hudson, 1988.

Parsons, Talcott. *Politics and Social Structure.* New York: Free Press, 1969.

Pilger, John. *A Secret Country: The Hidden Australia.* New York: Knopf, 1991.

Plant, Roger. *Sugar and Modern Slavery.* London: Zed Books, 1987.

Pryce-Jones, David. *Graham Greene.* Edinburgh: Oliver and Boyd, 1963.

Rau, Bill. *From Feast to Famine: Official Cures and Grassroots Remedies to Africa's Food Crisis.* London: Zed Books, 1991.

Salvatore, Anne. *Greene and Kierkegaard: The Discourse of Belief.* Tuscaloosa: University of Alabama Press, 1988.

Sartre, Jean-Paul. *Being and Nothingness.* Trans. Hazel E. Barnes. New York: Washington Square Press, 1956.

———. *Existentialism and Humanism.* Trans. Philip Mairet. London: Methuen, 1948.

Schiller, Herbert I. *Culture, Inc.: The Corporate Takeover of Public Expression.* New York: Oxford University Press, 1989.

Solzhenitsyn, Aleksandr. *The Gulag Archipelago.* Vol. 1. New York: Harper & Row, 1973.

———. *The Gulag Archipelago.* Vol. 2. Trans. Thomas P. Whitney. Glasgow: Collins/Fontana, 1976.

———. *The Gulag Archipelago.* Vol. 3. Glasgow: Collins/Harvill, 1978.

———. *One Day in the Life of Ivan Denisovich.* New York: Bantam, 1970.

Spinoza, Benedict. *On the Improvement of the Understanding; The Ethics; Correspondence.* Trans. R. H. M. Elwes. New York: Dover, 1955.

Spurling, John. *Graham Greene.* London: Methuen, 1983.

Taylor, John G. *Indonesia's Forgotten War: The Hidden History of East Timor.* London: Zed Books, 1991.

Thomas, Brian. *An Underground Fate: The Idiom of Romance in the Later Novels of Graham Greene.* Athens: University of Georgia Press, 1988.

Vilas, Carlos M. *The Sandinista Revolution.* New York: Monthly Review Press, 1986.

Wolferin, Karel van. *The Enigma of Japanese Power.* New York: Vintage, 1990.

Index

Abraham, the patriarch, 90
Adams, Stanley, 56
Africa, 55, 82, 85
Amin, Idi, 122
Amos, the Hebrew prophet, 73
Arendt, Hannah, 37, 128
Argentina, 28, 68
Aristophanes, 107
Aristotle, 37
Armenians, 3
Arnold, Ida (*Brighton Rock*), 2, 4, 13, 14, 24, 36, 60–62, 66, 70, 88–89, 91, 95, 112–113, 118, 126, 128
Assistant Commissioner (*It's a Battle-field*), 15, 19, 20, 39, 71–72, 102
Aunt Augusta (*Travels with my Aunt*), 5, 11–12, 14–15, 19, 63, 80–81, 85, 87, 90–94, 123
Austria, 24

Baudelaire, Charles, 20
Beauty, 19, 72, 86, 102
Beer Sheva, 62
Belgian Congo, 33
Belgium, 33
Bellow, Saul, 2, 6
Ben Gurion University of the Negev, 62
Bergson, Henri, 20
Berkeley, 78

Bible, 26, 74, 93, 95, 105, 129
Bishop, The (*Monsignor Quixote*), 12, 47–51, 123
Bloom, Harold, 62
Böll, Heinrich, 4, 38
Bosnia, 77
Bourgeois, Roy, 40–41
Brighton Rock, 2, 4–5, 11, 13, 21, 27, 34, 55, 59–60, 62, 67, 70, 73, 88, 112, 126–127
Britain, 24, 79, 80, 103
British Monopolies Commission, 56
British Secret Service, 38, 40
Brown (*The Comedians*), 31, 62–63, 66, 69, 70–71, 74, 80, 89, 91, 95, 101–104, 109, 125
Brown, Pinkie (*Brighton Rock*), 2, 5, 11–15, 17, 21–22, 60–61, 67, 88–90, 112–113, 127
Buber, Martin, 18, 45, 47, 63, 74, 94, 111, 121
Burnt-Out Case, A, 2, 5–6, 12, 18, 45–49, 68–69, 75, 82, 116, 122–125
Bush, George, 78

Camus, Albert, 2, 5
Capitalism, 7, 13, 26, 33, 71, 81, 92, 94, 96, 110

Capitalist corporation, 12, 26, 28–29, 35, 94, 102, 104

Captain and the Enemy, The, 2, 12, 17, 30, 42

Caribbean, 34, 101

Carter, Jimmy, 28, 29, 100

Castle, Maurice (*The Human Factor*), 40, 95

Castle, Sarah (*The Human Factor*), 40, 95

Catholic Church, 47–50, 72, 89, 95, 107, 115

Catholicism, 45, 47, 86, 101

Central America, 34, 41, 77, 101, 117, 118

Cervantes, Miguel de, 47

Chaplin, Charlie, 47, 63

Chile, 28

China, 93

Chomsky, Noam, 4, 34, 78–79, 101, 117

CIA, 2–3, 12, 16–18, 23–25, 28, 30–31, 33, 40–41, 59, 88, 129

Cicero, 118

Clinton, Bill, 78

Colin, Dr. (*A Burnt-Out Case*), 46, 48

Comedians, The, 2, 5–6, 16, 23–24, 28, 31, 35, 55, 62–63, 69–70, 80, 83, 91, 99, 102–103, 109, 121–122, 125

Commonweal, 35

Communism, 35

Congress, 41, 77–78

Concasseur, Captain (*The Comedians*), 69, 104

Confidential Agent, The, 2, 6, 21, 55, 64–67, 72, 113, 115, 118, 124, 127

Conrad, Joseph, 7, 29, 33, 55, 80, 82; *Heart of Darkness*, 33, 55, 80, 82; *The Nigger of the Narcissus*, 7

Corporate capitalism, 13

Courage, 5, 18, 21, 42, 64–65, 69–73, 86, 100, 111–112, 129

Crimean War, 37

Cuba, 34

Cubans, 100

Cullen, Rose (*The Confidential Agent*), 2, 21, 64–68, 72–74, 107, 113–115, 118, 128

Cuoto, Mario, 35

Czechoslovak invasion, 35

Czinner, Dr. (*Stamboul Train*), 3, 24, 55, 60, 66, 85, 87, 91, 95, 107

D. (*The Confidential Agent*), 2, 55, 64, 66–67, 72–74, 95, 107, 113–115, 118, 124, 127–128

Daintry, Colonel (*The Human Factor*), 38–39, 109

David, the Biblical king, 74, 95, 129

Decalogue, 89, 99, 122

Dialogue, 18–19, 31, 45, 47–48, 58, 65, 73, 86, 88, 94–96, 102, 111–113, 116

Dominican Republic, 107

Dostoyevsky, Fyodor, 71, 81

Dr. Fischer of Geneva or The Bomb Party, 17, 24, 30, 56–57, 64, 76, 82, 91, 111, 127

Duvalier, François (Papa Doc), 23–24, 28, 35, 63, 70, 80, 83, 100, 122, 124

Eagleton, Terry, 61–62

Eichmann, Adolf, 36

El Mozote Massacre, 41

El Salvador, 34, 40–41, 100

Elijah, the Hebrew prophet, 73, 121

Else (*The Confidential Agent*), 66, 115

End of the Affair, The, 90

Engels, Friedrich, 26, 47; *The Condition of the Working Class in England*, 26

England, 37–38, 55, 79, 118, 124

England Made Me, 6, 11, 14, 22, 25, 29, 81, 91, 110, 122

Erdinast-Vulcan, Daphna, 23–25

Fascism, 38

Faulkner, William, 2, 29; *The Snopes Trilogy*, 29

First Samuel, 129

Fischer, Anna-Luise (*Dr. Fischer of Geneva or The Bomb Party*), 64, 76, 111–115, 118

Fischer, Dr. (*Dr. Fischer of Geneva or The Bomb Party*), 17, 30, 56–57, 64, 70, 87, 91, 111–113, 124, 127

Fort Benning, 40

Fortnum, Charlie (*The Honorary Consul*), 41–42

Fowler, Thomas (*The Quiet American*), 2, 4, 13, 17–18, 24, 31, 36, 51, 58–60, 66,

75–76, 88, 95, 104–106, 116, 118, 124, 128
France, 6, 38, 79
Franco, Francisco, 27, 38, 48
Freedom, 1–3, 6, 12, 15, 19, 26, 30–31, 33, 37, 40, 47, 50, 55–56, 59, 69, 89, 92, 99, 104, 124

Gaza Strip, 62
Genet, Jean, 4
Geneva, 56
Genocide, 3
Getting to Know the General, 6, 16, 27, 73
Gordimer, Nadine, 38
Gramsci, Antonio, 16
Greece, 122
Grenada, 34
Guatemala, 28, 34, 100
Guevara, Ernesto "Che," 16
Gulags, 3
Gun for Sale, A, 35

Haiti, 16, 23–24, 34–35, 37, 55, 63, 70, 80, 83, 100–103, 125
Hale, Charles (Brighton Rock), 14, 60, 70, 89, 112–113
Hall, Jim (England Made Me), 22
Hamit (The Comedians), 71
Hargreaves, Sir John (The Human Factor), 38–41
Heart of the Matter, The, 20–21, 29, 51, 68, 85, 109, 127
Heidegger, Martin, 4, 116, 123, 126
Hemingway, Ernest, 2, 38; For Whom the Bell Tolls, 2, 38
Herodotus, 19, 26
Herrera, Father (Monsignor Quixote), 47–51, 123
Herrera, Omar Torrijos, 16, 27, 28
Herzen, Alexander, 86
Hitler, Adolf, 56, 61, 62
Hobbes, Thomas, 14–15, 18–19, 94
Hobbesian battlefield, 71–72
Hobbesian state, 127
Hobbesian system, 16
Hobbesian world, 14–16
Honduras, 34
Honorary Consul, The, 27–28, 41–42, 67
Hosea, the Hebrew prophet, 73

Human Factor, The, 38, 40, 42, 50, 95, 109

Indochina, 2, 34, 58, 73
Indonesia, 100
Intifada, 13
Islam, 46
Islamic jihad, 49
Israel, 2, 46, 62, 99
Israeli army, 2, 95
Israeli oppression, 13, 62
Israelis, 2
It's a Battlefield, 3, 15, 19, 27, 39, 71–72

Japan, 92, 93
Jefferson, Thomas, 29
Jeremiah, the Hebrew prophet, 73
Jesus, 59
Jones, Alfred (Dr. Fischer of Geneva or The Bomb Party), 57, 64, 111–112
Jones, Major (The Comedians), 63, 69–70, 80, 83
Joseph (The Comedians), 71
Joyce, James, 37; Ulysses, 37
Justice, 1, 7, 31, 37, 40, 60, 66, 71–72, 86, 92, 102–103, 116

Kafka, Franz, 6
Kant, Immanuel, 88, 94
Kennedy, Joseph, 41
Khomeini, Ayatollah Ruhollah, 122
Kierkegaard, Søren, 5, 15, 90, 115; Fear and Trembling, 90–91
King, Martin Luther, 16, 85
Kissinger, Henry, 19
Koran, 27, 93
Krough, Erik (England Made Me), 11–12, 14–15, 17, 19, 22, 25, 29–31, 90–94, 110, 122–124
Ku Klux Klan, 3
Kulaks, 3

La Prensa, 40
Latin America, 40–41
League of Nations, 56
Lieutenant (The Power and the Glory), 12, 18, 21, 49, 51, 95, 123
London, 71, 102
London Blitz, 111, 114

Love, 1, 17, 19, 20, 48, 64, 68, 72, 86, 102–103, 109, 111, 116
Luxemburg, Rosa, 16

Magiot, Dr. (*The Comedians*), 5, 16, 18, 21, 28, 31, 36, 62–63, 64, 66, 69, 71, 74, 80, 91, 95, 99–103, 106, 122–125, 129
Mahfouz, Naguib, 26, 27
Mandela, Nelson, 16, 85
Manhattan, 78
Manicheism, 89–90
Mann, Thomas, 2
Marx, Karl, 15, 47, 106; *The Communist Manifesto*, 47
Marxism, 101
Marxist materialism, 21
Marxist regime, 12
Mexico, 6, 38, 49, 72
Mexico City, 2
Middle East, 95
Ministry of Fear, The, 42, 69, 82, 95
Mississippi, 29
Monsignor Quixote (*Monsignor Quixote*), 47–49, 64, 76, 85, 93–95, 105–108
Monsignor Quixote, 12, 47–49, 123
Moses, the Hebrew prophet, 73–74, 99, 121–122
Muhammed, prophet of Islam, 59
Mussolini, Benito, 56
My Lai, 35

Navi, 99
Nazi Holocaust, 3, 116
Nazi Party, 116
Nazi SS, 3
Nazis, 11
Nazism, 62
Neruda, Pablo, 4
New York Times, 34, 117
Nicaragua, 2, 21, 28
Nietzsche, Friedrich, 6, 66, 101, 106–107; *Thus Spoke Zarathustra*, 101, 106
Nixon, Richard, 13, 19, 85, 122
Nizan, Paul, 69
North Vietnam, 35

Oklahoma City, 49

Oppression, 2, 12, 31, 35, 62, 77, 91, 93
Ortega Y Gasset, José, 111
Our Man in Havana, 17, 40, 109

Palestinians, 2, 13, 62, 95
Panama, 16, 24, 27–28, 38
Panama Canal Treaty, 28–29, 40, 55
Paraguay, 2, 11, 24, 27–28, 30, 34, 37–38, 55, 68, 80–81, 91, 122
Paris, 33
Parkinson, Montagu (*A Burnt-Out Case*), 12, 15, 18–19, 48, 90, 116, 123
Paul VI, Pope (Giovanni Batista Montini), 108
Pentagon, 40
Percival, Dr. (*The Human Factor*), 38–41, 109
Perez, Colonel (*The Honorary Consul*), 41, 67
Philippines, 28
Philistine, 129
Philipot (*The Comedians*), 69, 71, 103, 109
Phuong (*The Quiet American*), 31, 58, 104, 116
Picasso, Pablo, 42
Pineda, Martha (*The Comedians*), 63–64, 103, 109
Plarr, Edward (*The Honorary Consul*), 28, 41–42, 67–68
Plato, 20, 22, 24, 107, 111, 114, 116, 122, 124, 125; *Gorgias*, 22, 107; *The Laws*, 125; *Phaedrus*, 20, 107; *The Republic*, 24; *Theaetetus*, 111
Polis, 19, 122
Power and the Glory, The, 2–3, 6, 12–13, 18, 21, 46–50, 72–73, 90–91, 95, 107–108, 115, 123, 127
Proust, Marcel, 2
Pryce-Jones, David, 76–77
Psychologists, 3
Pulling, Henry (*Travels with my Aunt*), 11, 14, 19–20, 80–81, 87, 102, 125
Pyle, Alden (*The Quiet American*), 5, 12–13, 17–19, 24, 30–35, 58–60, 63, 76–78, 88–90, 93–96, 104–106, 116, 118, 124

Querry (*A Burnt-Out Case*), 18, 45–46, 48, 68, 82, 96, 122, 125

Quiet American, The, 2, 4–5, 17, 24, 30, 33, 35–36, 40, 50, 55, 58, 75, 77, 83, 88, 104

Quigly (*The Captain and the Enemy*), 2, 12, 17, 30, 42

Rabin, Yitzchak, 46
Reagan, Ronald, 19, 21, 37, 61, 77–78, 91, 108, 126
Roche, 57
Rome, 122
Romero, Archbishop Oscar Arnulfo, 16, 41, 100
Rose (*Brighton Rock*), 11, 14, 60, 88–89, 95, 112–113
Rousseau, Jean-Jacques, 56
Rowe, Arthur (*The Ministry of Fear*), 42, 69, 74, 82, 95
Rwanda, 3, 77, 80
Rycker, Andre (*A Burnt-Out Case*), 2, 5, 12, 15, 45–51, 69, 79, 90, 93–96, 123, 125
Rycker, Marie (*A Burnt-Out Case*), 12, 45–46

Saigon, 59, 75–76
Sancho (*Monsignor Quixote*), 47–48, 64, 76, 94
Sandinista regime, 21
Sartre, Jean-Paul, 2, 4, 12, 62, 67, 76, 86, 118
Saudi Arabia, 27
Saul, the Biblical king, 129
School of Americas Watch, 40
School of the Americas, 40–41
Scobie, Henry (*The Heart of the Matter*), 29, 51, 68, 85–87, 90, 127
Scobie, Louise (*The Heart of the Matter*), 20–21, 87, 109
Scriptures, 48
Shakespeare, William, 105, 115; *King Lear*, 105, 106; *Macbeth*, 115
Sinai, Mount, 122
Smiths, the (*The Comedians*), 63, 70–71, 80, 100–104, 125
Social scientists, 3
Socrates, 22, 62, 95, 107, 108, 111, 114, 116, 118

Solzhenitsyn, Aleksandr, 4, 16; *The Gulag Archipelago*, 16
Somoza, Luis, 2, 27
Sophocles, 51; *Antigone*, 51
South Africa, 16, 38, 40, 50, 85
South America, 28, 42
South Vietnam, 35
Soviet KGB, 3
Soviet Union, 3, 6, 15–16, 40
Spain, 38, 47, 55, 106
Spinoza, Baruch, 114, 116; *The Ethics*, 114
Spurling, John, 76, 77
Stalin, Joseph, 16, 61
Stamboul Train, 3, 6, 35, 55, 60, 75, 81, 85
Stein, Gertrude, 7, 19
Stockholm, 29
Stroessner, Alfredo, 24, 27–29, 122
Struggle, 1, 7, 12, 19, 70, 72, 101–102, 114, 116, 121, 125, 128
Stupidity, 21, 26, 95, 109, 115
Success, 1, 14, 18, 21–22
Sweden, 38, 91
Switzerland, 24, 56

Thatcher, Margaret, 37, 91
Third Man, The, 24
Third World, 3, 94
Thomas, Father (*A Burnt-Out Case*), 46, 79, 82, 91, 116
The Times, 35
Tokyo, 93
Tolstoy, Leo, 20, 37; *Anna Karenina*, 20, 37
Tontons Macoute, 3, 21, 23, 24, 35, 63, 70, 79, 103–104, 122
Travels with my Aunt, 5, 11, 19, 27–28, 30, 80, 87, 102, 123, 125
Trump, Donald, 126
Tse-Tung, Mao, 122
Tutsi, 80

Uganda, 122
Unamuno, Miguel de, 5
United Kingdom, 38
United States, 3, 6, 21, 23, 27–28, 30–31, 33–34, 36–38, 40–41, 46, 49,

58, 61, 75, 77–79, 80, 83, 85, 88,
    94, 100–101, 103, 117–118, 122,
    126

Vatican, 48
Vienna, 25
Vietnam, 2, 18, 28, 33, 35, 38, 55, 58,
    73, 75, 79, 88, 104, 118, 124

Warren, Mable (*Stamboul Train*), 75, 85
Washington, D.C., 28, 33
Washington Post, 34, 117
Watergate case, 85

West Germany, 40
Whiskey priest (*The Power and the
    Glory*), 3, 24, 50, 72–73, 90–91, 107,
    116, 127
Wilson, Edward (*The Heart of the Mat-
    ter*), 20–21, 109
Wolferin, Karel van, 92–93
Women, 2, 92–93
Woolf, Virginia, 2
World War II, 25, 93, 103

Yugoslavia, 38, 55
Yusef (*The Heart of the Matter*), 29, 86

ABOUT THE AUTHOR

HAIM GORDON is Associate Professor in the Department of Education at Ben-Gurion University of the Negev. He has published widely in philosophy and education and is the author of *Naguib Mahfouz's Egypt: Existential Themes in His Writings* (Greenwood, 1990) and *Make Room for Dreams: Spiritual Challenges to Zionism* (Greenwood, 1989); coauthor of *Sartre and Evil: Guidelines for a Struggle* (Greenwood, 1995); and coeditor of *Women's and Men's Liberation: Testimonies of Spirit* (Greenwood, 1991). He has been active in the struggle for human rights in Israel.